"Captivating and inspiring! Every morning as I sit with my coffee preparing for the day ahead, I read one poem or short passage from Julie Thayer's, *Made For This*. Each one of these thought-provoking works is just what I need to complete my morning routine, setting me up to move through my day, mindfully and purposefully. Julie writes in a beautiful poetic voice that inspires hope and optimism to embrace each day, whatever it may bring."
—**JULIE RUSSELL**, Educator, B.A. Hons, B.Ed & Associate Diploma, proud mom of two fabulous humans

"I love, love, love this book! It is so packed with positive insights to guide you through the 'Ick' and to understand that life is both this and that. *Made For This* is inspirational and helpful, the best kind of combination. Julie takes it beyond this and provides you with the map for actioning and creating your most authentic and aligned reality. This book is your pathway to nourishing your deepest experience of unwavering and unconditional self-love."
—**SUSAN HALL**, Portfolio Entrepreneur & Philanthropist, mother to three, grandmother to five

Praise for Made for This

"I have known Julie Thayer for over twenty years and can confidently attest that she is the real deal, having helped hundreds of women through her remarkable combination of knowledge, compassion, and love. Her extraordinary ability to communicate through words makes you feel you are walking alongside her on a journey of self-discovery, guided by a gifted, incredibly aware, experienced, and insightful mentor. This book needs to be on everyone's coffee table as a daily reminder that we all have the power to heal and grow. Julie's knowledge, her deep respect for humanity, and her inspiring approach make this book a must-read. The way this book is crafted is truly exceptional and reading it will undoubtedly leave you feeling uplifted and inspired. Julie's message resonates deeply, reminding us that love is always the greatest gift we can give ourselves and others."
—**SANDRA WILLIAMS,** National Account Manager,
  McNairn Packaging, youngest of nine siblings,
  and mom to two awesome daughters

"A refreshingly honest and loving perspective of the human experience. The heartbeat of the book resides in the nuances of courage and grace needed for whole health and healing. It's a breath of fresh air in an age of information overload because it's not only beautifully written; it's infused with sustainable guidance, motivating meditation, as well as powerful antidotes for feel-good living. All of which acknowledge how challenging it can be to face the uncontrollable contrasts in life, while assuring the reader of their resilience and that they deserve to thrive."
—**NICKI DI GRAVINA,** RHN, PMP,
  Owner & Founder of @feedforlove

"*Made For This*, by Julie Thayer, is an absolutely lovely read! It leaves you feeling like you've been wrapped in a blanket...in front of a glowing fireplace...held tenderly in the deepest of care and compassion. It's wonderful to feel like someone really understands what you have been through, and Julie's words offer profound resonance on repeat, affirming you are ok, you are not alone, and you've got this! There is a passage for every feeling you're feeling; the good, the bad, and the ugly, and it's literally like Julie is right there with you, by your side through it all, leading you forward with great wisdom and unrelenting encouragement to empower you to dig deeper and keep going! Thank you!"
—**DANIELLE VISCO**, Entrepreneur, CFO, Forest Ridge Landscaping, Real Estate Investor, Certified Yoga Teacher, mom of three amazing adult children

"*Made For This* isn't just a collection of beautifully written passages—it's a powerful tool you'll find yourself returning to time and time again. Depending on where you are in your personal journey, each chapter speaks to you in a way that's uniquely relevant, offering guidance, illumination, and clarity. Whether you're seeking self-discovery, inspiration, or simply a moment of reflection, this book is jammed with gems of invaluable, actionable insight for every stage of your growth and healing."
— **ANDREA WETZEL**, People Leader at lululemon

Made for This

Made for this

words to thrive by when life gets hard

JULIE THAYER

Copyright © 2026 JT Writes Life

By Julie Thayer

First Edition 2026

All rights reserved.

No parts of this publication may be reproduced, stored in a retrieval system, or transmitted in any form or by any means, electronic, mechanical, photocopying, recording, or otherwise, without the prior written permission from both the copyright owner and publisher.

ISBN: 978-1-7780654-2-2

Edited by Natasha Vera

Art Direction by Morgane Leoni

Disclaimer

All the information, techniques, skills, and concepts contained within this publication are of the nature of general comment only and are not in any way recommended as individual advice. The intent is to offer a variety of information to provide a wider range of choices now and in the future, recognizing that we all have widely diverse circumstances and viewpoints. Should any reader choose to make use of the information contained herein, this is their decision and the author and publishers do not assume any responsibilities whatsoever under any condition or circumstances.

Dedicated to:

You.

Even after all this time
the sun never says
to the earth,
"You owe me."
Look what happens
with a love like that,
it lights the whole sky.

—Hāfiz

Made for Wholeness – 3

Made for Awakening – 45

Made for Resilience – 79

Made for the Now – 153

Made for Connection – 189

Preface

Welcome to *Made for This: Words to Thrive By When Life Gets Hard*, a book designed to guide you through life's curveballs, to empower you to make the very best of the good bits, and to help you find hope and resilience in the midst of it all.

This book is made for all of us—me, you, and everyone who has ever felt the grip of life's uncertainties. If you are currently standing at a crossroads, overwhelmed by decisions, or facing challenges that seem impossibly insurmountable, let the words shared on these pages be your lifeline to capacity, serendipity, and newfound hope. If you've been feeling stuck, lost in the quicksand of self-doubt, uninspired by the world around you, or despair has made itself fully at home in your heart, you need to know that you are not alone on your journey. I've been there, too.

The lessons and revelations in this book, collected over time and literally compiled in the trenches of life, reflect my healing journey that began in 2017, spanning eight years and counting. Of special note, I was further inspired through my work as a Yoga and Pain Recovery Coach and the courageous clients whom I have been privileged to serve. Within these pages, you will find yourself engaged in an intimate conversation between my heart and yours, and it means the world to me that you are here for it.

This book tells the story of the greatest love affair you will ever have, the one you have with yourself. It's about embracing the dualities of life: the moments of wonder that take your breath away, in the best of ways—"The Awe"—and the difficult experiences that leave you feeling beaten and broken—"The Ick." Together, we will learn to expand with greater presence and connection into the moments of magic while also nourishing your capacity to meet the profound pain that inevitably accompanies a life well-lived. And, to do it all with grace and courageous resolve.

Every word and every aspect of this book is crafted with deep intention, with deliberate repetition to anchor key concepts and to support you in evolving a rich, robust inner dialogue and mindset. Even the white space is here on purpose—it is a place for you to write or doodle your reflections, insights, and feelings relative to how each passage resonates for you…or not. I have also shared several meditations. Please feel free to record the scripts to your device, so they are available to you as needed.

As you read this book, remember that just because a passage doesn't resonate today doesn't mean it won't tomorrow or six months from now. Life is fluid, and so are you. For your first read, I encourage you to experience this book sequentially as the chapters build upon one another, forming a timeline that invites you gently and purposefully into self-discovery and transformation. Moving forward, I urge you to revisit these words as part of your daily self-care routine; they are meant to meet you where you are and guide you on your unique path. My wish is that *Made for This* becomes a trusted companion on your journey, one that you can return to time and time again.

Remember, you are made for this journey of living, learning, and growing.

You can thrive, even when it's hard.
Thank you for being here.

With love,
Julie

chapter 1

Made for Wholeness

We feel because we live.
We live because we feel.
We love because we live.
We live because we love.

In your journey of wholeness, you will be asked to embrace your imperfections and the full spectrum of your humanity—your light and darkness, your joy and pain. You will emerge from the ashes fully empowered as you take responsibility for your well-being, cultivate self-awareness, and nurture your inherent worth. Through mindful actions and compassionate connection, slowly but surely, you will reclaim your life and discover that healing is always within your grasp. In this book, a safe, sacred space, you will explore honoring your boundaries, nourishing your soul, and loving yourself wholeheartedly. You will embody the truth of who you are and the place within you where authenticity can thrive.

The Gift

Repeat after me...

The responsibility of nourishing my whole health belongs solely to me and is a profound act of gratitude for the next breath I have been gifted.

Wholly

We are each the entirety of our perfectly imperfect humanness.

Our real and perceived vulnerabilities and weaknesses need not define who we are, or who we become, any more than our strengths and successes do.

We are this and that.

More often than not, our greatest abilities and talents are revealed through the opportunity of getting to know and taking care of the hardest, darkest parts of ourselves.

Through this process, you will grow skilled in the practices of:

- Self-awareness
- Self-acceptance
- Self-connection
- Self-compassion
- Self-respect
- Self-direction

Now is the opportunity to lean into your discomforts, your pain, your less than stellar moments of living, with gentle courage. It is the chance to learn more about yourself, so that you may meet, move through, and keep going in the stickier, ickier bits.

In the end, you will become a deeper, richer version of yourself through diligent daily habits of self-care and reflecting on the wisdom gained from your lived experience. All so that you may come to see your strengths with better clarity, evolve them, and step more fully into what expands you into your truest, most aligned self.

We are each the sum of our light and our darkness, our joy and our pain, our strengths and our vulnerabilities.

Wholly human, wholly loved.

Whatever It Takes

How do we ease anxiety and rise out of depression?

How do we take our lives back and reclaim our whole health?

We do so by choosing to do whatever it takes to empower our own healing and recovery.

We go inward, we practice awareness, attentiveness, we inspire deeper connection, and we initiate consistent, mindful, purposeful action.

Maybe you need to…

- Breathe differently.
- Delve deeper into mindfulness.
- Check out meditation.
- Move more, differently; do yoga, walk, run, bike, hike, try qigong, take up kung fu, salsa dance, play in the garden, paddleboard…whatever floats your boat.
- Eat differently; better, more, less.
- Nourish and hydrate.
- Sleep longer or sleep less.
- Talk more, and to the right people.
- Talk less and listen more, again, to the right people.
- Read more of the good stuff.
- Find yourself a counsellor. If it's not a good fit, you don't stop searching until you find the one that is.

- Check out group counselling and say YAY, this feels good, or NOPE, not for me.
- Consider medications that help you take the edge off, give you the space to cope, and to do what must be done to compel movement forward.
- Maybe you are already on meds and they are doing the job, or perhaps they are exacerbating current symptoms and/or creating new ones.
- Advocate for yourself and go to the psychiatrist to say, "Hey, I don't feel right."

All of the above, some of the above, or none of the above may be helpful in navigating your journey with mental health. What ends up working may completely surprise you. The fact remains that healing and recovery lies within your very own hands.

If you KNEW that a resource, tool, or lifestyle change could ease discomfort, sadness, and pain and move you towards contentment, joy, and freedom, would it not be worth giving it a try?!

And it goes without saying, some of the things you choose to explore in your self-care strategy may not always become part of the solution, but MANY absolutely will. Imagine your symptoms alleviating, maybe even disappearing—how freaking awesome would that feel?!

Your mental well-being,
your whole health,
go get it,
whatever it takes,
you are worth it.

Human

A life is to be discovered
and experienced; lived in,
loved in, learned in,
laughed in, cried in,
lost in, found in,
fallen in, risen in,
and everything in between.

Nourish

When we recognize, respect, and mobilize our self-worth, we bring deeper clarity, efficacy, and integrity to our boundaries.

And, in turn, consistently aligning with and upholding our boundaries fortifies our self-worth.

When we know and acknowledge our intrinsic value, we are motivated to create vigorous boundaries to support and honor ourselves.

When we maintain and protect our boundaries, not only do we exercise our courage and confidence muscles, but we also nourish and reinforce our self-worth.

Self-worth and boundaries need each other to work.

They are interdependent and inextricably linked.

So…

- Put yourself first.
- Get crystal clear on your non-negotiables in your relationships (both romantic and platonic).
- Practice both diligently.
- Foster connectivity by deeply leaning into all interactions.
- Enrich and expand into the relationship with yourself and others.

Commit to feeling good in all of your connections.

Home

Home is the place
I feel safest
to be who I am, as I am,
in this moment of
living and learning, so that
I may see, hear, and feel
the depths of my soul,
to honor its calling,
to love and be loved
without judgement,
to grow from this gracious space
of deep inner knowing and
unwavering personal integrity.

Feeling is not always easy work, but it is always worthy work.

Good Grief?

When we deny and dishonor our grief, to placate and prioritize the needs, expectations, and discomforts of others, we do ourselves a great disservice.

From the get-go, we are encouraged to expand into the goodness of our lives, to make connections, to be in relationships, to pursue our dreams, to live.

So, we do just that. We open our minds, our hearts, we take the plunge, we risk, we live and love—hard. It becomes the source of our joy, our pain, our purpose, and it's what brings meaning to our lives.

But, when we experience loss—when our tender hearts are broken, our souls shattered—we are expected to contain and shrink our grief, to pull our socks up and get on with it. Not only that, it is expected sooner rather than later, and so disproportionately to the magnitude of the void now present in our lives. It's ridiculous, really.

Grief is unique to each one of us, to each circumstance.

There is no normal.

There is no right way, no wrong way.

There is no shame in grief.

There are no rules.

There is no timeline.

It hurts, it sucks.

It's freaking uncomfortable, for everyone.

It never really goes away.

The only way is through.

And if we allow ourselves the time and space to meet and move through it—not forcing, not pushing, letting it ebb and flow through us—we will eventually find a little more peace, a little more capacity, a little more perspective. All while evolving and discovering gentle ways to keep going, to keep living, to keep loving, to keep growing.

Our pace, nobody else's.

To deny ourselves is to keep ourselves stuck in the thick of restrained grief, and the toll is, well, further mental, emotional, and physical suffering.

So, consciously choose to honor your process, and hold genuine space for others to do the same. This will allow for deeper grieving and, therefore, for the much-needed acceptance, connection, compassion, clarity, courage, healing, strength, resilience, grace, capacity, and belonging that come with it.

Let's recognize that grief is a naturally occurring, guaranteed human experience. Also, let's do a better job normalizing it, so we can all feel more comfortable with the prominent role it plays in our lives.

Your way is the way. Journey on, unapologetically.

You Deserve to Feel Good

Yes. You.

Life can feel hard sometimes, maybe even most of the time. And we forget what it's like to feel good. The longer this goes on, the more immersed we get in the sticky, icky bits. We see more obstacles than possibilities. We accept what *is* instead of imagining what could be, and feel less deserving of living any other experience.

The fact is, meeting the ups of life is pretty effortless—we don't generally need strategies and problem solving skills to navigate the goodness in our lives. The good stuff is self-propelling and tends to, by its very nature, empower feelings of joy, peace, hope, connection, capacity, success, freedom, and fulfillment.

The downs, however, can be a different story. We aren't really taught how to meet, cope, and move through the tough stuff. We don't have honest, deep conversations about loss and grief, and the prominent role they play in our lives, nor how to take care of ourselves and each other when they inevitably happen. It's more of a Hail Mary, throw spaghetti at the wall to see what sticks, kind of scenario. We fumble our way through and try to be strong and stoic in the face of it. We try to get on with our lives, without really giving ourselves the time, space, and grace, to process, to understand, to heal, and to keep expanding into our human experience, despite the void. Instead, pain, in its various expressions, takes root and weaves its way into all aspects of our daily existence, insidiously leading our nervous systems into perpetual survival mode—stuck on "freeze"—and denying us the feel-good.

What we so often fail to realize is that we were made for this and what we need to thrive in life's ebb and flow exists within us. When we intentionally tap into it, it's transformative.

Invitation to Grieve Your Way:

Your grief, your way.

Honour your process.

Take all the time and space you need to make sense of your new reality.

Feel it in every way it needs to be felt.

Let it breathe and be in the fabric of your being.

Accept it will always be a part of you, with the power to shape your todays and tomorrows.

It will remain a tender echo sheltered in your mind and heart.

It will always be there to remind you that loving deeply and living fully is both risky and worth it.

When healing happens and the time is right, you will make your way back to hoping, loving, and living, with the recognition that, through your lived experience, you have actually made room for MORE.

The Whole Enchilada

Never mistake vulnerability for fragility.

Our capacity to be vulnerable, to open up our hearts and minds to the whole enchilada of the human experience, takes, shall we say, big cojones!

The oh-so-sweet reward of leading ourselves mindfully and bravely through our vulnerabilities and fears is a rich and expansive way to love and live.

So…

Love BIG.

BIGGER still.

Grant yourself the grace to live and learn, perfectly imperfectly.

Stay curious.

Do the intentional work.

Have fun with it.

Get out of your own way.

Aim for authenticity and alignment.

Choose to reconnect with your passions and purpose—daily and deeply.

THIS IS WHO YOU ARE.

Trust, believe, and have faith your instincts will lead you in the direction of integrity, wholeness, and healing.

Set yourself free...give flight to your dreams, your desires, and know with your whole heart that you are most deserving of LIVING YOUR BEST LIFE.

Fearless?

No.

Courageous?

Yes.

The Ick

It makes absolute sense that, when we are suffering in our bodies and minds, we tend to orient our mindset to what's wrong with us. We focus intention and energy on enduring our discomfort, and ruminating on how it prevents us from participating in the "doing of life."

It's human nature to be wired to the negative, driven by our survival instinct. When this instinct is triggered in modern society—where we are no longer required to outrun lions, tigers, and bears—we find ourselves held hostage by a nervous system working on overdrive to keep us safe. We find ourselves stuck in a loop that perpetuates and escalates our distress.

What if, alternatively, we began to perceive and receive the presence of pain, disease, and illness as a powerful message from within?

What if we practice tending to the whispers of imbalance before they are amplified into their fullest expressions—commanding our attention, leaving us no choice but to deal—at which point it's really freaking hard.

What if we could intentionally and compassionately engage with our pain?

What if we could open our hearts and minds to the possibilities that exist when we become more aware and connected to our pain experience?

What if we could shift our language around it, so we could lead ourselves forward and through it from a place of empowerment?

What if we could moderate our nervous system through aligned action? We can focus on our breath, movement, mindfulness, meditation…the list goes on.

What if we asked ourselves, "What can I do?" versus telling ourselves on repeat, "I can't do…"

We can either lean into what we feel has been taken away from us, or we can lean into what remains and expand into it. Choosing the latter gives us a far better chance at inspiring a more desirable outcome, don't you think?

And this is not about fixing or curing ourselves, it's about creating as much capacity, grace, peace, joy, contentment, love, and life as possible. All while we work on healing, recovery, and restoration.

You can feel better, even in The Ick of it.

Through

PAIN, unheeded, be it physical, mental, or emotional, becomes a sneaky, slow bleed that, if left unattended, morphs into an epic, far more unmanageable, Herculean hemorrhage.

Turning our backs on it, tucking it away into some deep, dark crevice within us, does not negate it or make it disappear.

The alternative?

We choose to meet it. Compassionately.

To sit with it, especially the messy, yucky bits.

To bravely face it and do the tougher work.

We go lovingly inward.

We slowly, steadily, intentionally peel back the layers to lead ourselves home to wholeness and healing.

We set ourselves free and reclaim our peace…our lives.

We go through it.

It's the only way.

Healing is not easy work and it is the best work you will ever do.

Self-Care

Self-care is self-respect.
It's that simple.
From how we breathe, move,
play, rest, eat, drink, think, talk,
to the choices we make, relative
to the company we keep
and the experiences we seek.

Lighthouse

See your light
Know your light
Trust your light
Love your light
Live your light
Shine your light
Share your light

Bravely
Brilliantly
Abundantly

Your light
is nourishment
for the world

Take Care

Take care, as in really
take care of yourself,
today and every day,
in every possible way.
You are that important.

Life Happens to Us All

There are certain circumstances, situations, and outcomes over which we have little or no control.

Just as we experience the ultimate joy, we experience the depths of despair, heartbreak, trauma, loss, and grief.

How is it, then, that we might meet this inevitable life conundrum with capacity and equanimity?

How can we not only survive but thrive?

How do we find bliss in the process of becoming?

We choose it.

We choose intention.

We choose perfectly imperfect.

We choose compassion.

We choose to nourish, to nurture, to keep our buckets full—our breath, body, mind, energy, and soul.

We choose mindful will over what we can control.

We choose to strengthen our muscle of resilience.

We choose to wonder, to keep our hearts and minds wide open.

We choose to feel both the light and the darkness, receiving and processing our present moment pleasure and pain.

We choose to understand and speak our truth, with clarity and conviction.

We choose to act on our passions and purpose, to serve.

We choose to lead, courageously with love, for ourselves first, then others.

We choose to succeed.

We choose to fail.

We choose to sit in gratitude for limitless growth and teachable moments.

We choose to practice all of the above, daily, diligently, deeply.

We choose to keep going, to embrace the bittersweetness of being.

In this place.

In this space.

At this time.

We grow.

We expand.

We choose to leave a legacy that ripples and resonates, graciously, infinitely, beyond our last breath.

You Are The Artist

When we begin to perceive, receive, and accept ourselves as whole beings—versus fragmented and broken—our eyes open to the masterpiece behind the strokes of paint. When we invite the integration of our hurts and heartaches, and welcome the growth that comes from lessons learned, we amplify our capacity for whole health healing and recovery.

You are your very own masterpiece.

- Growing
- Glowing
- Laughing
- Loving
- Living

Return home to yourself, reclaim your wholeness.

Your magic is infinite.

Ask yourself: *What would the best version of me do today?*

Wholeness Meditation

Fear becoming courage.

Limiting beliefs becoming aligned, empowered action.

Clarity becoming purpose.

Receive these words, as they may be meaningful to you, in this moment of your life.

Breath in.

Breath out.

Feel their possibilities.

Feel their power.

Invite connection.

Invite intention.

Invite integration.

See and feel the wholeness of your being.

Breathe in.

Breathe out.

Store the memory of this peaceful vibration away, within your physical tissue, so that you may recall it in times of doubt.

Take a deep breath in, fill your belly, rib cage, chest.

Let your breath go…big, beautiful sigh out.

One more time—big breath in, bigger breath out.

Ahhhhhhh……

Carry on brave, resilient human.

Passage

One moment turns into two,
two into five, five into thirty, thirty into sixty...
An hour into two, two into five, five into twenty-four...
A day into two, two into five, five into three hundred and sixty-five...
A year into two, two into five, five into ten....

When we lean into it,
when we make space,
healing happens.

Breathing gets easier
grief softens,
pain eases,
perspective comes.

We learn to integrate our lived experience,
we rediscover capacity,
peace,
joy.

We find a way to keep going,
to keep growing,
to live and love,
more,
and again.

To heal effectively and sustainably, we must first feel safe.

The Critic

Talk yourself into healthy, happy, and whole.

Consciously choose this to the very best of your ability, in any given moment. Especially in those tougher moments, when your unrelenting, misguided inner voice is revving turbo-style and fiercely determined to convince you otherwise.

Take a breath, dig deep, silence The Critic, and intentionally shift the dialogue to one of kindness, compassion, patience, love, and truth.

Talk to yourself like you are the love of your life.

You are!

How you speak to and of yourself is a powerful daily habit that can fuel your wellness or unwellness.

- Choose your words wisely.
- Don't rely on assumptions to inform your reality...doing so can lead you straight into the rabbit hole and, the deeper you go, the harder it is to claw your way out.
- Embrace your perfectly imperfect self.
- Give yourself the grace to keep learning and growing.

You are a human BE-ing, showing up for yourself in a very challenging world...in this alone you are enough.

Stories

What stories do you tell yourself, about yourself?

Choose your words wisely, honestly, respectfully, compassionately, and lovingly.

Guess who is ALWAYS listening?

Invitation to Practice Kind Conversation with Yourself:

Take the next two minutes to write everything you LOVE about yourself right now, from the teeniest-tiniest thing to the BIGGEST. If you are struggling to do this—because yes, this can be hard—I want you to pay attention to the less-than-stellar thoughts and flip them into a single affirming statement that reflects their complete opposite.

For example:

"No matter what I try, I fail at it, it all just falls flat, and I wonder why I even make the effort."

Ouch.

How about this, instead?

"I have been so adventurous and courageous in my life and tried many different things. Not everything has worked out according to plan, and that's ok... I have learned a lot and I am using this wisdom to get clarity, refine my plan, and make better decisions. For this reason alone, I am always growing and experiencing success."

Awesome.

Wash. Rinse. Repeat.

Baby Toe Steps

Aim for healthy, happy, and whole, each and every day...breath, body, mind, energy, and soul.

What supportive, subtle shift/choice might you make today to cultivate greater contentment...peace...freedom...?

No need to kick any doors down here...pick one small thing...make it realistic...doable...have fun with it...practice it until you become it and when you do...celebrate!

Then, work on your next opportunity and baby-toe step it all the way into existence!

REPEAT.

REPEAT.

REPEAT.

By doing this, you are empowering new pathways, new habits, and new experiences.

You are inspiring sustainable, healthy, happy, and whole living.

You deserve to feel good.

What can this look like?

As part of my acute healing journey, I made a point of walking as often as I could, meaning pretty much daily, despite the weather. Everything about it felt hard; my mind and body were heavy and there were tears often. From the beginning to the end, with each baby toe step, I recited the mantra…"healing, recovery…"—it felt like an effort in survival. However, I chose to keep moving, surrounded by nature, breathing in the fresh air, and absorbing the vitamin D. The days turned into weeks and the weeks turned into months and I could literally feel the slow, steady healing of my mind, body, and soul. Today's mantra is…"growth, gratitude, growth, gratitude, growth, gratitude…"

Warriors

If we choose to embrace life fully, there is absolutely no way we are making it through this short, sweet, sassy adventure unscathed.

We are also well aware that not a one of us is going to make it out of this wild, wonderful, and wicked ride alive—another tough pill to swallow.

We will inevitably take risks—some calculated and some are the eyes-squeezed-shut, not-even-sure-there-is-water-in-the-pool-but-I'm-still-launching-off-the-high-platform-diving-board kind of risks.

We will be both rewarded—LIFE ROCKS!—and relegated—BACK TO THE BENCH!—relative to the myriad of our decisions, actions, and efforts.

At times, we will joyously celebrate our good fortune, maybe even sit back to simply savor the sheer exquisiteness of breathing, being, loving, and living.

However, there will be days, maybe even months or years, where we feel battered, bruised and broken. Like warriors, engaged in a tireless battle—fighting for worth, understanding, acceptance, kindness, compassion, forgiveness, freedom, health, sanity, and humanity—fighting for our lives.

Wounds may run deep, become part of us—ignorantly and "blissfully" tucked away—buried over time beneath layers of scar tissue; namely distraction and dysfunction. And we all know what happens to unattended wounds—they fester and eventually serve to nefariously bite us in the ass!

How, then, do we get off the merry-go-round? How do we heal ourselves and learn to meet life head-on?

We slow it all down. We look in the mirror, practice honesty, and unveil our masks. We tend to our hurts, we start talking, we share the journey, and we own our shit. We begin to make peace with ourselves—mindfully, authentically, patiently, and lovingly.

WE DO seek external support, if healing and recovery exceeds our current capacity to help ourselves.

WE DO initiate thoughtful, purposeful, and necessary decision-making. We decide to scale the wall of our self-imposed prison.

We commit to our worth.

We do the work.

We set *ourselves* free.

Habits

There is a fine line between wellness and unwellness.

That line is drawn by the consistency and quality of our daily habits.

Choose wisely.

Choose lovingly.

Choose YOU.

YOU are worth it.

The Devil We Know

Empowering feel-good living often means gaining real clarity around what does not serve us; physically, mentally, emotionally, energetically, and soulfully.

It means making the conscious choice to look through the lens of our core values and detach from those daily habits we know are misaligned.

Easy-peasy, right?!

We wish.

It's effing hard.

There is a bizarre comfort in the devil we know.

It lures us in, under the guise of keeping us safe.

In reality, it shrinks us, preventing us from meeting the discomfort of change, of being brave, of speaking our truth, of feeling worthy of a different experience, of being the very best version of ourselves.

The truth is, sustainable healing and growth takes time…and so much more!

It takes love.

It takes courage.

It takes commitment.

It takes consistency.

It takes discipline.

It takes daily diligence.

It takes practice.

And the best part?

It is possible!

Letting go creates space for new and improved daily habits of wellness that help us feel integrated, whole, and ready for "even deeper" living and loving.

With each step, we come home to ourselves.

Choose you, for you, first and foremost. You benefit—everyone benefits—when you are consistently actioning the most loving, compassionate, capable, courageous, and optimal expression of you.

What steps can you take to ditch your devil?

1. Get clear on one core value you hold.
2. Reflect upon one daily habit you know does not align with this value. This may be health, lifestyle, or relationship related.
3. Think about the choices and actions you could take to shift this habit of unwellness into a habit of wellness.
4. Practice these things every single day until you feel yourself fully embody it mentally and physically. Until it becomes you.
5. Keep in mind, the latest research suggests it takes sixty-six days to create a habit. So give yourself time to make the change and trust it will be worth it!
6. Work on one "devil" at a time and repeat this process for each.

As an example, I value kindness and found myself in a friendship where I came to realize our discussions centered mostly on gossip and the judgement of others. It was really uncomfortable for me, it just didn't feel good and it was definitely misaligned. For a long time, I didn't speak up, because, firstly, I somehow hoped it would get better, but it didn't. And secondly, I didn't want to hurt my friend's feelings or be judged myself. Eventually, it became too unbearable and I chose to be honest with my friend, as kindly as I possibly could. Unfortunately, it inevitably resulted in the end of that relationship, but, in the long run, it brought me greater contentment to live in my integrity.

Living in alignment brings more confidence, capacity, clarity, peace, freedom, and feel-good living.

Moonlight on Water

I see you there darkness

To know you is to also know my light

You are but one precious piece of the puzzle

You do not define me, any more than my light does

We are one, whole

Dark, light, and all shades in between, dancing with wild abandon to the beat of this ever-fluid life

Juxtaposed in sweeping, startling contrasts, promising richer, deeper experience

To feel you darkness is to recognize that I have learned and loved and lived in this life, profoundly

This is your gift

Ricochet

Your inner demons—the ones that like to run amok, ruthlessly ricocheting between your heart and your head—capture them with great care in the palm of your hand. They feel smaller there, more manageable. And remind yourself, you are not defined by your oh-so-vulnerable, extra special guests. They are simply pieces of you, yearning for your undivided attention, respect, kindness, compassion, patience and love. Choose to see them, hear them, feel them, hold them tighter, and love them harder. Choose to mindfully move together towards greater self-acceptance, understanding, integration, wholeness, and healing.

chapter 2

Made for Awakening

It is time,
to stir from your soul-weary slumber,
to awaken in your innate and infinite power,
to consciously champion your metamorphosis,
to emerge from your chrysalis,
to unfurl your wings,
to fly.

Embrace each struggle as a stepping stone toward more courage and clarity—this is your opportunity. It is in the dance of your vulnerability and strength that you discover your voice, ignite your passions, and inspire a life that transcends self-imposed limitations. This journey is not about perfection; it's about the profound beauty of becoming—where healing meets intention and the ordinary transforms into the extraordinary.

Knock Your Socks Off

Let's face it...we are all on the ride of our lives. But it is only we who can determine its breadth, width, height, depth, capacity, direction, speed, steepness, and trajectory. Only we can answer the following questions...

Do I keep moving safely in the same circles or do I boldly traverse the inevitable peaks and valleys of whole-enchilada living?

Do I shift into turbo-mode and risk colossal derailment or do I hang tight in my seat and risk complacency, immobilization?

Do I hold on tighter, fighting fiercely with all my might, or do I release and let go willingly, consciously?

Do I hold my breath until I burst, maybe even stop breathing altogether, or do I breathe deeper and slower, or maybe harder and faster?

Do I feel the fear and practice courage, despite it?

Do I silence my voice or do I scream at the top of my bleeping, bloody lungs?

Do I laugh until I cry or cry until I'm tearless?

How about all of the above?

Welcome folks to the ride of your life and thank yourself for bravely climbing on board. BUCKLE UP, LOCK AND LOAD, because this ride...THIS RIDE...is going to knock your effing socks off!

Glimmers

When we are knee deep in struggle, believing in better days ahead may, at best, feel elusive, at worst, downright impossible.

The beautiful truth is, the silver linings slowly reveal themselves. A little shimmer here, a glimmer there, gently coaxing us forward, toward healing and a more authentic, fulfilling way of breathing and being in the world.

It is the well-earned reward of showing up for ourselves in the tough and uncomfortable, and choosing to lovingly meet and move through our pain. One breath, one brave baby toe step at a time.

You are strength.

You are courage.

You are worthy.

Hang on.

Keep going.

Trust.

Seek support.

You are not alone.

Safe

Healing happens when we...

- Feel safe
- Hold intentional and compassionate space for the moderation of our nervous system
- Slow things down, slower still
- Breathe deeper, longer
- Move our bodies kindly, gently
- Carefully unpack layers of living to reveal the deeper truth of our pain
- Mindfully soften into the discomfort
- Meet it
- Move through it
- Release it
- Expand beyond it
- Forgive our perfectly imperfect humanness
- Grant ourselves the opportunity to keep living and learning, to keep growing and going

Healing happens when we choose it for ourselves.

Invitation to Make Space for Your Healing:

In what ways are you currently feeling unsafe within yourself? Lean gently and compassionately into your vulnerabilities. Consider the choices you could make to foster a greater sense of security and stability, so that you can intentionally make space for your healing. Then give yourself the opportunity to practice being curious about your pain, versus fearful, judgemental, resentful, or neglectful. Open your mind and heart to the message(s) your pain is trying to convey to you. Reflect on what's rising up for you and what aligned action(s) you may consistently take to moderate your pain, to lead yourself through and beyond it.

Decide Today is the Day

Today is…

- The day you choose to honor the fire that burns in your belly.
- The day you choose to trust your intuition and answer your calling.
- The day you choose to unapologetically speak your truth and amplify your voice.
- The day you choose to show up in service, propelled by your passion and purpose.
- The day you choose to own your expertise, to lead, courageously, competently, and lovingly.
- The day you choose to touch the lives of others, to make your difference in the world.
- The day you choose to take intentional, aligned action, towards all of the above, because not doing so has literally become far too painful.

Make today that day!

Connect to My Calling Meditation

Take a breath in, notice your inhale, then a breath out, and notice your exhale. Draw your awareness to the rise and fall of your belly and let yourself explore five easy rounds of breath. Then, shift your focus inward to the depths of your belly and ask yourself, What compels me, drives me, inspires me, and lights me up?

Continue to breathe with spacious ease—oxygen in, carbon dioxide out. Let the answers simply bubble up with each filling of your belly. Receive the insights and feel that fire simmering within you ignite. With each softening of your belly, release the fears, the limiting beliefs, the inner conversations, and the external influences that rear deceptively to thwart you in the pursuit of your most precious dreams and desires. And lovingly remind yourself: no judgement, only compassion and gentle awareness.

Now, let yourself sit safely and bravely in the flames of your soul's most profound calling. Breathe in deeper clarity…breathe out any lingering doubts. Take your time here. And when you feel ready to do so, speak your truth, out loud, with conviction. It may sound something like this; "My purpose is…," "I am most passionate about…," "More than anything I want to…," "I will expand unapologetically into my expertise, which is…," "I am worthy of living in my fullest potential and that looks and feels like this…."

PS: I would highly encourage you to journal out your discoveries here. Have some fun with this! This is how you can make today that day of taking aligned action towards actualizing your highest vision for yourself.

Answers

We may not have all the answers we seek today...and that's ok...we don't need to.

We must, however, continue to show up with steadfast determination to keep creating and inspiring possibilities.

We must trust that, with each breath received and every new day gifted, we are moving towards greater clarity, confidence, and contentment.

How to Show Up with Steadfast Determination:

1. Acknowledge your more challenging feelings as they are, without judgment, and allow yourself to sit in their discomfort with compassion and curiosity. Do not rush this process to meet someone else's timeline or expectations.
2. When you feel ready, begin to tenderly explore the possibilities that may now exist as a result of your lived experience. What have you learned about yourself? How might you utilize the wisdom you have gained to make alternative or better choices, to shape and form your life differently, more intentionally, and authentically? Let these answers lead you home to yourself and into greater clarity, confidence, and contentment. When life happens, it invites the opportunity for powerful refinements within us if we let it.

What does this look like in action?

When I was in the hospital recovering from my suicide attempt in November of 2017, my psychiatrist suggested that I begin a journal, a seemingly innocuous request. However, I am an introvert and extracting the thoughts swirling about in my head, making sense of them, and getting them to land on paper was nothing short of excruciating. My first attempts, in my opinion, were abysmal and resulted in pages being ripped out, torn to bits, and dismissively tossed in the trash. My doctor gently encouraged me to keep going…to ditch the self-judgement and my need for it to be some sort of literary masterpiece…to simply keep writing. So, I did. And let me tell you, the dam broke. The words began flowing, and they haven't stopped since.

MORE

Let's consider the possibility that pain is
actually an invitation to restore balance,
to choose differently, to learn more about ourselves,
to live with deeper awareness, connection, and alignment,
to honor, love, and respect ourselves, more.

Neutrality

There is no shame in pain, be it physical, mental, or emotional.

So often we judge our pain experience, shaming ourselves and assigning a negative feeling and energy to it that, quite frankly, exacerbates and perpetuates its chronic, debilitating presence.

What if, instead, we perceived our pain from a place of neutrality and not as the enemy?

What if, instead, we received our pain with an open mind and a compassionate heart?

As a whisper from within, an insightful messenger, as to where an imbalance may exist within our brain, body, and nervous system.

Not as a problem, but as a possibility—a catalyst for much-needed connection and constructive change.

Not as a showstopper, but as an opportunity for mindful, purposeful action—aligned action that compels us forward, toward our optimal state of being.

Sweet Spot

All that we need to navigate this magical, maniacal ride of life exists within us. Accessing it, however, can be tricky. It requires daily, diligent practice in awareness, attentiveness, connection, acceptance, mindfulness, and aligned action.

When we settle fully into that sweet spot—that emboldened part of us that allows us to competently surf the edge where Awe and Ick meet—and when we get clear on and master our daily habits of wellness, we greatly amplify our capacity to live the moments of our lives with heightened discernment and intention. We get practiced at holding ourselves, simultaneously, in a state of steadiness, strength, grace, gratitude, effort, ease, adaptability, perspective, integration, and wholeness. Or what I like to call, "Living life in the pink!"

And, it is from this place that we may safely play in the realm of possibility, courageously and constructively leading ourselves forward, toward empowered, deep-rooted healing, growth, and living.

Our world can bloom beyond our wildest imaginations.

Better Me

When I consistently go inward to meet myself...

- I honor my present moment experience.
- I gain greater self-awareness.
- I inspire deeper connection.
- I empower aligned action.
- I master my inner world to confidently and constructively meet and integrate my outer world.
- I create more clarity and less confusion.
- I maximize my peace and minimize my suffering.
- I fortify my capacity for maneuvering life's ups and downs.
- I find greater flow, freedom, and fulfillment.
- I become a better me through the practice of my lived experience.

Do the Feeling, Receive the Healing

What one emotion are you really feeling today?

If it is positive in its vibe…receive it, sit in it, savor it, accept it, honor it, move with it and through it, and be oh-so-grateful for it. This means you are living your life.

If it is on the less than stellar side of the spectrum…yeah, crummy…receive it, sit in it, savor it (yucky bits and all), accept it, honor it, move with it and through it, and be oh-so grateful for it. This also means you are living your life.

Acknowledge all of your emotions—these "delightful" visitors passing through—with equal awareness, attentiveness, non-attachment, non-judgement, kindness, compassion, patience, love, and gratitude.

It is human nature to feel, so FEEL, dammit, ALL OF IT!

Choose to practice Present Moment Processing (PMP for short—ha ha!) to keep your harder, trickier, more mischievous emotions softer, smaller, and more manageable. And no more tucking them away for a rainy day, only to fester, get bigger, and sucker punch you later.

Do the feeling, receive the healing.

Knowing Better, Doing Better

In any given moment, life is a culmination of our choices and experiences.

What if, instead of jumping out of a perfectly good airplane without a plan and a parachute, you get really clear on your core values, and from these same values you:

- Make intentional, informed decisions.
- Empower your boundaries by having the conviction and courage to ask for what you need, and to walk away from what feels misaligned.
- Build a strong relationship with your intuition by leaning into that gut feeling, and trusting it to lead you forward from a place of deep connection and clarity.
- Practice taking action on what you can control and releasing the rest.

Now, reality check, doing all of the above doesn't always yield the outcomes we desire.

Why? Because we don't make decisions in a bubble.

This life thing can still feel a lot like trial and error, with success, failure, and everything in between up for grabs.

And there are aspects that simply remain outside our control.

However, what is guaranteed—if we choose to keep our hearts and minds open—is the opportunity to keep learning, growing, and expanding into our experience. To keep adapting and adjusting our choices, relative to what we now know. This is where our true power exists.

Knowing better.

Doing better.

Loving better.

Living better.

Invitation to Get Clear on Your Values:

1. Settle into a quiet space and allow yourself to reflect on the experiences in your life that have felt most aligned and fulfilling.
2. Relative to each experience, tap into the feeling that rises up for you, really let yourself sit in it and ask yourself, *What specific value led me to this experience and feeling?"* Maybe it's abundance or peace or productivity or....
3. Hone in on three to five core values, for optimal focus and impact. Creating clarity around your values is the first step in starting to build your intentional living foundation. These values, your non-negotiables will keep you grounded in your WHY when the going gets tough.
4. Have fun with this!

To inspire your process, I will share the core values that inform my decisions and actions:

I lead with LOVE and GRACE, in all that I am, in all that I do. I choose to share my authentic story, in written word, and to speak my TRUTH, so that others may be empowered to do the same; courageously, freely, and safely.

Tap Into It

Where does empowerment come from?

What's its source?

Where does it exist in endless supply, accessible 24/7?

It's called self-empowerment for a reason.

Let's explore how you can get to a state of empowerment using all the tools you have within you.

- Go inward.
- Practice authentic awareness and compassionate connection.
- Consistently tap into physiological feedback, your inner dialogue, intuition, mood, mindset, and energy… informing yourself as to the state of your being in any given moment.
- Collect data and make mindful, subtle course corrections to effectively navigate the now.
- From this place, taking aligned action and choosing daily habits of wellness over unwellness…on repeat.
- Lead yourself forward in a direction that propels expansion and allows you to meet the ebb and flow of life with confidence and capacity.

These brave choices will cause you to feel…

∞∞∞∞∞∞∞

- Grounded
- Growing
- Flowing
- Steady
- Balanced
- Curious
- Capable
- Free

∞∞∞∞∞∞∞

It's within you.

SANTOSHA

Complete acceptance and contentment.

How elusive does this feel when we are in the throes of battling depression and/or anxiety?

Contentment? Yeah right, good luck with that.

We are far too busy engaging in self-deprecating inner dialogue, convincing ourselves how "not enough" we are—not lovable enough, worthy enough, strong enough, smart enough. We are convinced that we are failing, somehow, at pretty much "everything," and that things will never, ever feel better.

The difficult part is that, when we are down and/or anxious, the stories we tell ourselves lack perspective, objectivity, and are not an accurate reflection of what we are truly experiencing, within and around us. As I like to say, we get sucked into the negativity vortex, and the longer we hang out there the harder it is to claw our way out.

What can be helpful is learning to catch ourselves engaging in negative self-talk, and shifting the story we are telling ourselves to one that is honest, fair, positive, and kind.

In a nutshell:

Choose negative self-talk's opposite.

Believe IT to be true.

Play IT on repeat, instead.

For example, "I am enough, and these are all of the reasons why...." Give yourself the opportunity to cultivate a sense of worth and contentment, even on your most difficult, dark days.

Change the narrative, change the experience.

Sweet Seat

Gratitude is our capacity to be fully present in each living moment of our lives.
Joy happens here.
Pleasure happens here.
Love happens here.
Forgiveness happens here.
Connection happens here.
Healing happens here.
Growth happens here.
Enough happens here.
Living happens here.

Taking time to sit mindfully in the sweet seat of gratitude is one of the most powerful ways to inspire healing and recovery, by bringing awareness to what does feel good in our lives and leaning into it more. That being said, it can be a little tricky to access, when we are in the throes of navigating physical, mental, or emotional pain.

So, start simply, steady as she goes, with the small stuff…a sunny day…a cuppa joe in your favorite mug…sharing a warm smile…indulging in Reese's peanut butter cups, YES, definitely these—ha ha!

Start by layering little bits of thankfulness upon thankfulness, to propel purposeful, present moment living, with your ever-emboldened, hopeful, brave, and grateful heart.

Gratitude When It's Hard Meditation

Pause.

Take a breath...this is possibility.

Look within and around you.

Pick just one thing.

Become fully aware of it.

Connect to it deeply.

Receive it fully into your being.

Let the waves of gratitude flow through you.

Let them lead you forward into your next moment of living.

Especially when it's feeling hard.

Good Mornings

What's your daily wake up routine like?

Do you pause to acknowledge that first conscious breath you take?

Do you take a moment to celebrate yet another day of living, loving, and possibility?

Or...

Do you reach for your phone and dive deep into scrolling?

Or...

Do you step onto your yoga mat or take a walk and allow yourself to settle into your physical, mental, or emotional being? Practicing awareness, deepening connection, inviting spaciousness and softening edges, before moving full throttle into your day.

Your daily habits have the potential to shape both your present moment and future moment experience. If your habits serve you well, they become trusted tools to empower sustainable feel-good living. They give grace, gratitude, equanimity, capacity, resilience, freedom, hope, and so much more!

You may choose daily habits of wellness or you may choose daily habits of unwellness.

The choice belongs to you.

And your daily self-care rituals don't have to be perfect. It's more about showing up consistently for yourself, present and purposeful.

What will you choose today?

Hint: CHOOSE YOU.

I can't emphasize this enough. There is time to be found in the morning, before the rest of the household and world wakes, before you are required to be present and "on," when the likelihood of you committing to a regular self-care routine is so much greater.

Hit Pause

Living an intentional life is not just about the "doing," it's also about making a habit of hitting pause, so that we may sit consistently in mindful reflection.

Being intentional means settling into that place of deep self-awareness and self-connection, checking in, and taking inventory of both our inner and outer world. We do this to ensure that our actions continue to meet and match our values, our goals, our wants, needs, desires, our dreams.

Let's ask ourselves on the regular:

- Am I happy, why or why not?
- Am I where I wish to be in my life?
- Am I in relationships that feel good, aligned, and safe?
- If I could change something, what would it be, how might I begin to create that shift?

As we learn from our lived experience, as we inform ourselves through our successes, failures, and everything in between, it is up to us what we do with this newly acquired insight and knowledge.

It is here where our true power exists.

It is here where we can choose stagnation or we can choose expansion.

It is solely up to us to keep our fingers on the pulse of our lives.

Courageously and constantly, evaluating, redoing, realigning, and reinventing.

Evolving.

Growing with purpose on purpose, leading ourselves forward into the most authentic expression of who it is we wish to be, in this moment of our lives.

Clarity comes with experience, if we let it.

Hindsight is twenty-twenty, as they say. It is only of real value if we choose to learn from our past, not beat ourselves up for not knowing better back then.

Know better. Do better.

When we breathe and get in alignment, we battle ourselves less, and we invite more integrity, more peace, more joy, and more freedom.

We inspire more loving, more living, more EVERYTHING.

Wander

Nature is a powerful healer.

Breathe it in,
ingest it,
immerse yourself in it,
however and whenever you can.

Go for a wander.
Find yourself lost and found.
In its wonder.

Only You

Only you can know your truth.
Only you can choose your truth.
Only you can speak your truth.
Only you can live your truth.

Change Maker

Live your life
led by love
on purpose.

In pursuit of your dreams,
propelled by your passion,
today and every day.

You are the magic
the world seeks,
you are the Change Maker.

Each new day brings with it a plethora of possibilities.

Decide to Thrive

What if, right now, you are completely lost in patterns of self-destruction and chaotic living?

Maybe you accept the chaos because it is the only reality you know.

Maybe you are afraid to trust that any other experience or outcome is possible.

Maybe you believe that life is meant to be painful, that you don't get to want anything more for yourself.

You accept.

You endure.

You survive…barely.

With your mind hurting.

Heart hurting.

Body hurting.

Your nervous system is on high alert, keeping you safe, protecting you from making any decisions, even those that may lead you into feel-good living.

Your daily habits perpetuate the myth that you are only worthy of suffering.

You stay stuck, on repeat.

What if the opposite were true?

What if what you deemed to be impossible was possible?

What if living in contentment, joy, peace, and love was your birthright? No more, no less than anybody else's, but yours.

What if you could shift the story?

What if you could transform your daily habits and expand infinitely into the life you desire and deserve?

What if, in doing so, you create a ripple effect that makes your life and relationships richer, deeper, more rewarding, more authentic, MORE of everything life has to offer?

What if, today, you decide to thrive?

chapter 3

Made for Resilience

Self-care,
diligently practiced,
over time,
is the fine line between
light and darkness.

Resilience beats in the heart of our lives, a testament to our ability to rise out of our disappointments and thrive in our comebacks. Let's get you reacquainted with your indomitable spirit within. Yes, you have one! Your spirit embraces challenges as gateways to growth and transformation, cultivates courage in the face of adversity, and turns each discomfort into a powerful catalyst for living your most vibrant and purposeful life. It is possible!

I See You

If you are seeking a reason
to keep believing, to keep going,
to keep fighting, to never give up,
then may this message find you
and remind you…

You are loved.
You are not alone.
You are worthy.
You matter.

Never, ever, forget this.

We Are Made for This

Life is this and that.

Calm and chaos.

Joy and pain.

Suffering and hope.

It is how we choose to meet, move through, learn from, align with, and act on each experience that determines the trajectory of our lives.

It is determined by how we lean in and expand, regardless of the Ick.

It is determined by us loving our way through it…with the deepest compassion for self, and for others.

It is determined by us remaining curious.

We create our destiny by holding steadfast to the wonder and enchantment of this human experience, even when it's hard.

We decide what kind of life we have by empowering freedom, flow, and fulfillment.

Only we can live our best life in the precious time we have been given.

Only we can trust...

We are *made for this*.

Invitation to Connect to the WE:

Take this moment to look *everywhere* for the presence of wonder and enchantment (WE) in your life.

Use all of your senses...

Do you see the daintiest flower breaking resiliently through a concrete sidewalk?

Do you hear the tinkling of wind chimes dancing delightfully on a gentle breeze?

Or maybe you're watching marshmallow clouds forming lovely shapes in the sky above?

Or waking to the smell of coffee wafting its way toward you, gently beckoning you into your day?

Or tasting the yumminess of oh-so-sweet chocolate melting marvelously in your mouth?

Or the feeling of a loved one's arms wrapped tightly around you in the biggest, squishiest hug?

Hold each discovery in your mind, in your heart, in every cell of your being. Notice how it feels to bring awareness to it. Can you describe your feelings? For example, does it bring you sadness or make you happy? I'm guessing on the happier side?

Now, allow yourself to sit in your experience of this found WE for a little longer. How does it land in your body? Can you describe the sensations? For example, does it make you feel heavier or lighter? I'm guessing on the lighter side?

When we are reminded that wonder and enchantment never cease to exist, even when life feels really freaking crappy, we can find and hold steadfast to these glimmers of light in the dark.

Sourcing our very own lifeline of joy, hope, gratitude, and possibility that weaves its way in and around our pain, gently coaxing us forward into healing and into living.

Bearing witness to the magic that exists, always, and for all time, a universal connection that binds us generationally in our shared humanity, compelling us to keep going no matter what.

In the WE, we are one.

Loving reminder: It can be particularly tough to connect to WE when we are sloggin' it in the Ick, so if this is you, right now, go easy with yourself. Start small, start with one, let this be enough. You can build from there.

In my early days of healing my WE was the sunrise; waking to it, that first conscious sip of air—of life—the gift of another day and the chance to try again.

Leave No Stone Unturned

If today your struggle is acute…

Pause
In this moment
Breathe

As long as this is possible, the healing you seek is possible

Gently move your body, in all the ways you are able

As long as this is possible, the healing you seek is possible

Bring loving awareness to your thoughts

What is your mind telling you?

Is it being kind, truthful?

Say to yourself, with conviction, on repeat…

"I am worthy. I am deserving of feel-good living."

As long as this conversation is possible, the healing you seek is possible

Be more kind
Be more loving
Be more patient…
with yourself

Keep hoping
Keep believing
Keep trusting...
In yourself

Ask for help

Source the right support for you

Leave no stone unturned

You are not alone

A gentle reminder...sustainable healing takes all the time YOU need.

We cannot change the past and, yes, we must own it, all of it, the good stuff and the tough stuff, but what we can do is learn from it, using the hard lessons "gifted" in our yesterdays to make better choices in our todays.

Darkness is Afoot

You find your perch, you set your grip, you insidiously weave yourself around every cell of my being

You hold me captive, blindfold, and bind me, there is no light, I am immobilized

You lick your lips in maniacal delight, steadfast satisfaction, as you make child's play of my vulnerability and shame

You taunt me, fastidiously devouring my heart, my mind, my soul, without care or conscience

You take what you want, leaving me vacant and bone-weary exhausted

You are relentless in your pursuit; complete annihilation is your endgame

You are my most ferocious foe, my nemesis

It takes all I have to greet you, to rise up and meet you, like the mighty warrior I know I must be

I fix my stance and bravely lift my sword, inevitably it falls, it feels heavier this time, I feel so encumbered I must draw upon my full arsenal of resource

Years of self-reflection, self-work, digging even deeper this time, hoping beyond hope it is enough

I fight fiercely and ache for a new dawn

Days turn into nights, nights into days

This battle, our battle, is epic

In one last hurrah, I anchor myself in gratitude, my battle cry is love, and I triumphantly raise my sword to strike an almighty blow against you

You don't expect it, it hits with precision, and you falter just long enough for that first glimmer of light to break through

It is enough for me, and I strike again, and again, and again

Today, you are beaten, the victory is mine I see you now, as you are

You are not real

You are not real

BUT I AM

Resilience

Some of the very best moments in life happen when we consciously choose to make ourselves vulnerable, not recklessly, or with wild abandon, but rather with reasonable care, mindfulness, and a very healthy dose of courage.

Many of humankind's greatest stories, triumphs, discoveries, and inventions have been yielded when hearts and minds have been cracked wide open, leaps of faith taken—all in the name of possibility and the proverbial "what if?" All while risking judgement, ridicule, and rejection.

It is in these raw and real moments of self-exposure that we tend to dream bigger and set loftier goals, where creativity is ignited, and hope is exponential. Does it work out every time? That's a big HECK NO-ha! ha! But when it does, oh man, the living is sweeter than we ever thought possible, and, well, that's a big HECK YEAH!

So, when risking it all has us landing splat, flat on our face, feeling battered, bruised, and broken, we absolutely do give ourselves time to rest, to heal, but only so we may replenish and rise up, refreshingly informed by our lived experience. So, we may, with our heart on our sleeve, continue to expand bravely and capably into our truth and into the fullness of our being.

The act of living is designed to be a perfectly imperfect adventure, and we are here for such a short while. So, stop being so hard on yourself and instead stay curious...never stop dreaming, exploring, playing, and practicing.

Keep trying.

Keep learning.

Keep connecting.

Keep aligning.

Keep evolving.

Keep feeling.

Keep loving.

Keep living.

You are worth it, and the world seeks just your kind of magic!

∞

What can this evolution look like?

- Get back to that hobby you used to love!
- Learn that new language or skill you've always wanted to!
- Try line-dancing, hip-hop, ballet, jazz!
- Take a course!
- Brainstorm this for yourself, then choose it and do it!

Saving Ourselves

What if we recognize we are not actually here to save one another, but rather to be here for each other, so we may feel consistently and compassionately seen, heard, and held through the inevitable ebb and flow of life?

What if we are a persistent, loving presence in each other's lives? Holding space, nourishing genuine human connection, and building a mutually stable foundation for living—a springboard—from which we may each safely and bravely meet and move through the Ick, to overcome it, to expand beyond it.

When we have the opportunity to practice leaning into the discomfort, the pain, the loss, the grief, we get better at it. We build trust and belief in our own capacity to heal and grow through the tough stuff, to live more, to love more.

To save ourselves.

Reminder, we save ourselves when...

- Our core values inform our choices and actions consistently. *This is alignment.*
- We honour ourselves and others when we consistently practice the mutual respect of clearly communicated boundaries. *This is a healthy relationship.*
- We courageously speak our truth and ask for what we need. *This is authenticity.*
- We don't give our time and energy away and prioritize other's needs at the expense of our own worth and well-being. *This is self-love.*

Invitation to Reflect:

Take a moment, kindly ask yourself: Is there room for improvement on this front? What would that look like? In what specific ways could you expand intentionally into these aspects of your life? How would it feel to experience more alignment, healthy relationship, authenticity, and self-love? Pretty darn good, I'm thinking!

Right Side Up

We may not realize it, sometimes, but our lives need a shaking up.

Perhaps, we have become complacent, settled into habits and routines that may have served a purpose, at some point, but no longer do so.

Or maybe it's fear of the uncomfortable and unknown that keeps us entrenched in unhealthy relationship patterns, or stuck in a job that is completely unfulfilling, or self-sabotaging through destructive decision-making.

And sometimes, a choice is made for us; our partner ends the relationship, we get overlooked for a promotion, maybe even fired, or we find ourselves facing a life-altering illness.

More often than not, it is a culmination of some version of the above that leads to what appears to be the *catastrophic implosion* of our lives. We are brought to our knees, waging a war we never saw coming.

This pull-the-carpet-out-from-under-us, complete and colossal leveling, shatters our world as we know it and leaves us enduring what feels like the ending of all endings.

No feeling better, no recovery in sight, just the Ick.

BUT, what if it is actually the beginning of all beginnings?

What if these uninvited upheavals become the catalyst for greater self-awareness and self-connection?

What if it is a veiled invitation to live and love more…and better?

What if it is offering the opportunity for deeper inner knowing, for further refinement and for fortifying a rock steady resilience, where *more awe* abounds and where our human spirit prevails.

Allow yourself to believe just enough in this idea of breaking down to break through, that you find *just enough will* to keep going…to survive…to thrive…again and again.

Sometimes, it all needs to be turned upside down, so that we may discover our new and improved right side up.

From the Inside Out

When was the last time you really smiled from the inside out?

Settling into your smile—your real deal smile, the kind that reaches your eyes and shines straight outta your heart, yeah that's the one!—may feel virtually impossible especially when moving through a period of deep sadness, pain, loss, grief, and trauma.

In fact, in the early stages of recovery, you may find yourself grudgingly practicing the half-smile as a strategy for in-the-moment crisis management. Smiling can support an instantaneous positive energy shift. Research has shown that the action of curling the corners of your lips up, even if you don't really feel happy, induces a physiological response similar to genuine happiness in the body. You might use this to navigate conflict and challenging situations with greater grace and ease, where you may typically lose your s*#t!, and in the words of Social Psychologist, Amy Cuddy, to "Fake it 'til you become it." I love, love, love the intention and spirit of this declaration!

I can certainly attest to exploring and experiencing all of this, relative to my own healing journey over the years. A cherished friend once asked me, "Can you choose happiness right now, in this moment, when life is really freaking messy and turned on its head. Can you simply accept it as it is and still find and feel joy?" And I didn't skip a beat responding, "Yes. Yes, I can and I have."

In some of my darkest, loneliest times I have come back to myself with a smile; fully, authentically, albeit fleetingly. And, it has been in those moments of complete acceptance and gratitude that I have been gifted these glimmers of joy, of hope, of possibility. And, as it turns out, the welcome and celebrated building blocks for living my life inspired even in the ickiest bits of it!

Lemons

Meet, manage, and move through the
soul-shivering sour bits.

Let your eyes scrunch shut,
your face crinkle,
your shudders shake you.

Acquire a kind, compassionate
taste for the discomfort.

Squeeze out the learning,
plant the seeds,
fill your cup with care.

Add ice for the refresh,
a dash of sweet-lived experience,
a sprig of mindful mint,
a thoughtful stir,
drink up…
AHHHH, this is living!

Gratitude, even for the tough stuff, is a powerful promoter of healing and growth.

Chain Reaction

It rarely serves us to hang out for too long in the extremes of our behavior—from how we eat, drink, move, and sleep, to how we work, play, love, and live.

Seek harmony, hold space for the yang and the yin, those complementary and opposing forces we encounter along the way; light and darkness, joy and pain, love and loss, doing and not doing. What others come to mind?

Practice mindful moderation, so that you can exist, most consistently, in the sweet spot of your experience…physically, mentally, emotionally, energetically, and soulfully.

Practice meeting the ebb and flow of life with grace and equanimity.

Nourishing your inner world nourishes the entire world.

Invitation to Practice Mindful Moderation:

Can you think of areas in your own life where there is opportunity to bring more balance and harmony?

From your brainstorming, pick one specific shift you would like to make and then decide upon one choice or action you can take today to support its actualization. Practice it every day for the next sixty-six days, until it becomes part of your being.

Congratulations, you have just transformed a daily habit of unwellness into wellness!

Repeat this process as soon as you feel things getting a little topsy-turvy...before it gets too big and unmanageable.

Overthinking

Overthinking is a consequence of getting stuck in the loop of trying to control the uncontrollable in your life...over and over and over again.

It can lead you into taking misaligned action or into complete immobilization.

It can have you functioning from a foundation of fear and frustration, feeling anxious, hopeless, and helpless.

How can you shift overthinking into peace of mind, intentional problem-solving, and constructive productivity?

The answer is simple (we humans have a way of making rocket science out of everything!), but that doesn't mean easy: if you practice diligent self-awareness to determine what is within your control and what is not, guess what, thinking gets a whole lot more sensible, purposeful, and doable. Hasta la vista monkey mind!

Choose It. Do It.

FACT: It takes way more energy to overthink and talk ourselves out of self-care than to take the self-care step itself.

We generate reason after reason why we can't show up for ourselves...distractions, excuses, limiting beliefs, and fear. Not to mention the time and energy we then commit to beating ourselves up for breaking promises to ourselves...cue the feelings of lack, not enoughness, guilt, shame, self-flagellation, and disappointment. Round and round we go, fueling a self-fulfilling prophecy that leaves us running on empty and spiraling into full throttle burnout.

In the time it's taken us to convince ourselves to practice self-neglect, we could simply choose it and do it...as in, we are already doing it, getting it done, and, before we know it, deriving the benefits! And guess what? Decisive, aligned action creates results, and results create more decisive, aligned action. This, in turn, propels hope, possibility, and progress.

You want to walk in the morning? Lay your clothes out the night before, then get up, get in them, and get out the door!

You want to hit the gym after work? Minimize the obstacles! Grab your gear, put it in the car, so you can head straight there! Less time to entertain "Should I, shouldn't I?" More time for "I can, I will."

Lead yourself forward with a momentum that serves you and say hello to self-worth, acknowledgement, acceptance, connection, respect, responsibility, satisfaction, and capacity.

Lean into this exponential growth, instead!

Whatever your self-care practices make them non-negotiable.

Make choosing you, over and over again, the habit you can't live without!

Just One Thing

If you could pick one daily habit, that you know does not serve you well, and shift it into a daily habit of wellness, what would it be?

And, what if, right now, in this moment, you decide to make that change for yourself? To choose it, to do it, today, tomorrow, the next day, the day after that…and again, and again, and again…

On average, it takes more than two months before a new behavior becomes automatic—sixty-six days to be exact.

Pick just one thing, practice it.

Creating one new and improved habit has a ripple effect, physically, mentally-emotionally, and energetically. The benefits snowball in the most wonderful of ways, the feel good is contagious, and other shift happens…it amplifies, effortlessly, organically, because you literally come to crave more of the goodness that comes from intentional, aligned living. You come to trust yourself more. You come to realize, you, yourself, are capable of empowering a different outcome.

And, if you fall off the wagon (it happens!), forgive yourself, recognize your perfectly imperfect humanness, and try again, keep going…keep leading yourself forward. Start again, new minute, new hour, new day, new week….

You deserve mindful, resilient, rich, whole health and well-being.

∞∞∞∞∞∞∞∞∞∞∞∞∞∞∞∞∞∞∞∞∞

- Pick just one thing
- Don't overthink it
- Choose it
- Do it
- Over and over again
- Expand into it
- Embody it
- Watch it grow and become MORE

∞∞∞∞∞∞∞∞∞∞∞∞∞∞∞∞∞∞∞∞∞

You are worth it!

TRY

Try
intentionally
courageously

Fall down?
it's ok

Rest
do the feeling
receive the healing
grow

Try again
more informed
more intentionally
more courageously

Fall again?
it's ok

Rest
do the feeling
receive the healing
grow some more

Try again
even more informed
even more intentionally
even more courageously
and this time

savor the success
the win
the reward
the actualization of
your resiliently pursued
goals and dreams

Celebrate big
do the feeling
receive the healing
grow even more

Keep trying
keep falling
keep rising
keep living
keep learning

Don't stop

Keep freaking going

Tipping Point

There are times we may find ourselves precariously perched at a tipping point.

When we feel as likely to fall back, arms and legs a-flailing, into oblivion, as we do to fall forward, with arms and legs a-flailing, into possibility.

There is a third option, and that is we hold calm, strong, and steady in the present moment.

How do we do this?

We breathe in, we breathe out.

We root with our feet firmly planted upon the earth.

We rise, drawing length to our spine and side body, a little drawing of the belly button into the back body to engage our deeper core.

We intentionally hug our musculature in toward the bones of the body, enough to support stability, and we soften, enough to invite playful exploration.

We bring a broadening to our collar bones, we feel our shoulders softening and our hearts lifting, the back of our necks lengthening, our jaw relaxing, our cheeks, the space around our eyes, the temples and forehead, too, the crown of our head reaching skyward.

Each deliberate action makes more space for breath and lifeforce energy to flow, for nourishment to flood every cell of our being, for clarity and wisdom to surface.

From this safe, supported place, we focus solely on the moment in front of us.

We intentionally choose to nudge the edges of our experience… one step forward, two steps back, followed by three steps forward, one step back, and so on, and so on, until we find ourselves mindfully, sustainably, re-aligning and progressing, think the little engine that could, with lessons learned and endless growth inspired.

This is the daily practice.

This is how we find the resolve to dance with our discomfort.

How we remain diligently curious in the face of what it is we don't know.

How we live and love, courageously and capably, truly and deeply.

Consistency

What's one thing you will do to nourish your well-being today?

Choose it.

Do it.

Make it non-negotiable.

What happens when you do it consistently?

- [ ] You acknowledge and affirm your worth.
- [ ] You create a daily habit of wellness over unwellness.
- [ ] You build a competency in showing up for yourself.
- [ ] You begin to realize you do possess the power to give yourself what you need.
- [ ] You come to rely upon and trust yourself.
- [ ] You foster self-connection over disconnection.
- [ ] You fill your cup and fortify your capacity to meet the good stuff and the tough stuff with space and grace and resources.
- [ ] You discover healthy habits multiply, one becomes two, two becomes four...
- [ ] You create momentum and feel-good living becomes self-propelling.
- [ ] You learn, you grow, and your life gets richer and deeper.
- [ ] You facilitate outcomes and results that align and amplify.
- [ ] You lead yourself forward one daily habit at a time.

So...what's your one thing?!

Get to it.

You are worth it.

The In-Between

Embracing the day-to-day demands of life, whilst attending to healing and recovery, can be both invigorating and exhausting.

It is really hard work.

What makes it so? "Empowered you" begins to make choices, and slowly but surely life begins to shift.

This is also when the rubber meets the road—when it becomes even more important to hold tight to your truth.

Why?

Because you are in what I like to call the In-Between, that place where you feel yourself being energetically compelled forward; an inspiring and liberating place, where you begin to witness extraordinary possibilities unfolding around you, things that make you say, "Hey, I am definitely on the right path here."

On the flip side of this is the devil you know, your past. Although you know it does not serve you well, there is a bizarre security in it, a false reality, that insidiously draws you into retreat mode.

Tread very carefully here.

This is where you will be required to dig deep, to hold steadfast to your truth. If you are an empath, this is going to demand everything you've got, as there may be some in your circle who feel lost or deeply hurt, despite your best efforts to act with care and compassion, by the changes within you, and the actions you are taking. It is here you may be inclined to not only hold space for your own healing, but you may overwhelm yourself with sincere, heart-driven attempts to take responsibility for their experience too.

DANGER. DANGER. DANGER.

If you do find yourself hanging out in the In-Between it's time to batten down the hatches and hold steady as she goes. Yes, you may find yourself heading toward parts unknown, and, yes, that can be positively terrifying—I feel you, yes, I feel you. But this is the moment you choose to believe with your whole heart that you deserve the magic that awaits you in the Land of the Unknown. Not in the form of rainbows and unicorns, but rather in the form of freedom and fulfillment. The reward of not giving in, when the deceptive pull of perceived "safety" feels a whole lot easier, is the adventure of living your truth.

Besties

Can you name your deepest fear?

Can you meet it with curiosity?

Can you hold it with kindness and compassion?

Can you lovingly embrace it?

Can you make it your bestie?

Can you stop fearing your fear?

Work with it?

Learn from it?

Cultivate courage with it?

Inspire growth with it?

Fuel capacity with it?

Lead with it?

Love with it?

Serve with it?

Make your difference with it?

YES.

YOU.

CAN.

Empowered fear + intentional living = infinite possibility.

Affirm: "I am not fearless, but I am brave."

YES.

YOU.

ARE.

White Knuckles

Our daily habits are controllables that fuel function or dysfunction. Either way, we empower our results through the consistency of our choices and discipline.

What's the opportunity here?

If we choose mindfully, with intention, and we practice aligned action diligently, over time, we can create more of the life we desire.

So what if we traded in the unpredictable *fly-by-the seat-of-our-pants* approach for a more thoughtfully curated living strategy? One that supports our capacity when life's uncontrollables have other plans for us, as they often inevitably do.

We would start functioning formidably and persistently from a place of connection, purpose, passion, and trust.

No more white knuckling it.

We are the answers we seek.

The Best Work You Will Ever Do

When we are struggling with pain be it physical, mental, or emotional, what do we often forget to do?

Our first instinct is to seek the answers and support outside of ourselves.

We seek the quick fix, the Band-Aid solution that addresses the symptoms, but not the underlying cause.

Whatever gets us back to "doing" as quickly as possible, and to what we believe is functional.

For a little while, anyway.

We are then surprised and frustrated when we find ourselves sidelined, yet again, by the return of symptoms and our pain amplified.

Round and round we go, feeling greater helplessness and hopelessness, and falling deeper and deeper into the rabbit hole.

More discomfort, more pain...less feel-good, less living.

So what's the missing piece?

We neglect to go inward.

We neglect to understand the daily habits that lead us into our manifestations of discomfort, pain, depression, anxiety, illness, and disease.

And yet, it is here where the magic really lives, where our true power exists.

When we become aware, connected, and aligned, we fuel our capacity to meet and move through our pain on a whole new level.

From the inside out, sustainably.

From this place, we become a participant in our own recovery, and it is from here we magnify the impact of the relationships with our team of healthcare professionals.

The inner work can feel like the scariest and hardest work we do, but trust me when I tell you, it's the best work you will ever do.

Take massive, mindful action towards your mental well-being and whole health management.

Courage

Feeling afraid is a natural, instinctual response to real or perceived danger. It has value, it has purpose, it has significance; survival being number one.

When we have a choice, relative to our non-life-threatening fears, what matters most is how we mobilize ourselves, physically, mentally, emotionally, energetically, and soulfully, to intentionally and bravely move beyond our fears and into possibility.

Gathering experience, inviting expansion, empowering growth.

Fearless? No.

Courageous? Yes.

We can survive and thrive.

Invitation to Nudge Your FEAR

When we inform our decisions through our fear—False Evidence Appearing Real—and our limiting beliefs, yes, we may keep ourselves safe, but we may also keep ourselves stuck. So, we are going to hang out in this discussion for a bit, because learning to dance gently and compassionately with fear is a powerful growth catalyst!

Let's begin our exploration with a little story of what this can look like:

> *It was in a hospital bed in December of 2017, while recovering from my suicide attempt that inspired me to start Julie Thayer Yoga. I recall thinking to myself,* How can I take this catastrophic life event and make a difference, do some good with it?
>
> *In that moment, I decided that sharing my experience would not only support my own healing, but allow me to show up in service to others who may also be struggling. I remember asking myself,* Julie, this is going to mean a very raw and real unveiling, can you do this? Can you live with what this may invite? *I was so worried that I would be judged and very afraid of unkind comments and feedback. Not only that, I wondered,* were people even going to care about hearing my story? Did it really matter?
>
> *I sat with it, for literally less than a minute, and immediately flipped all of it into the following mantra, "If it helps one person make a phone call, to reach out for help, then the occasional vulnerability hangover will be more than worth it." And it has been, a thousand times over. And I can honestly say there has not been a single unkind comment, only compassion, love, and an ever expanding community.*

So, now we are going to go toe-to-toe, in the most loving of ways, with your fears and limiting beliefs. This is among one of my most favorite exercises to explore with my clients, where fear is emboldened and untapped potential is discovered and set free. Think of it as the best treasure hunt upon which you will ever embark.

Firstly, let's get some clarity on limiting beliefs.

What Are Limiting Beliefs?

1. We create limiting beliefs because our less-than-stellar experiences and history have marked us with a sense of lack and vulnerability, and the story we create, based upon minimal evidence and maximal assumptions, becomes our truth.
2. If left unchecked, limiting beliefs amplify into a perceived threat, activating the fight-flight-freeze-fawn response, and serve to perpetuate a vicious cycle of unnecessary self-protection.
3. Over time, we cease to trust ourselves, negating our intuition, undermining our self-confidence, and convincing ourselves that the answers we most desire are to be found elsewhere.
4. We keep searching. We keep repeating. We feel stuck…over, and over, again.
5. Limiting beliefs then become excuses and make us reliant on others and circumstances over which we have little or no control.

What's the alternative? We…

- Go inward
- Meet the fear
- Sit with it
- Acknowledge it
- Evaluate it
- Build a relationship with it
- Empower it
- Learn to use fear to our advantage

How are we going to do this? Well, you've got homework!

In this offering, you will:

1. Learn how to surrender your self-created fears, limiting beliefs, and obstacles to catapult yourself into your fullest potential. This process begins with the White Sheet Meditation.
2. Learn how to construct a healthy, positive relationship with fear—one that mobilizes you into mindful action. Because not doing so, not leaning into your passion and purpose, is more painful than the fear itself.
3. Understand that fear is good. Fear matters. It means you care and that your passion and purpose are awakening.
4. Learn to meet your fear and use it to propel you forward, to amplify your life and your capacity.
5. Learn how to show up authentically and confidently in all the layers of your being...to own it!

What's Next?

- Lead yourself through the White Sheet Mediation. See script below.
- Ensure you are in a quiet space with no distractions.
- Take the time to move through the meditation in its entirety.
- Give yourself the grace to sit with everything that comes up for you during this meditation.
- Afterwards, take out your journal and let all the words, feelings and ideas that bubbled up flow onto your paper.
- Who was present for you at your four corners of the sheet? Who wasn't? Do you feel a newfound clarity relative to your support system?
- What specific limiting beliefs and fears were gathered and set free? How did that feel for you in breath, body, mind, energy, and soul?
- Don't hold back here, get all your limiting beliefs out, and think about what would be possible for you if those limiting beliefs did not exist.
- Reflect upon how you may transform your fears into intentional, empowered action.

White Sheet Meditation

Take some time to settle into your space, be it seated, lying down, whatever feels just right for you. Get as comfortable as you possibly can. Bring a gentle awareness to your breath, as your body surrenders heavily into all points of contact between your body and the earth. Inhaling, exhaling, softening, and surrendering. Feel your breath slowing down, feel your body letting go just a little more with each passing round of your breath. Feel your mind getting lighter and calmer. Open your heart and mind to possibility, to receiving the words and guidance. Alternative: Feel yourself soften into the space between your brows, this is your mind's eye.

The sun is high in the sky and you feel its warmth upon your skin. The sky is a rich blue and you find yourself immersed in the whimsical sights and sounds of nature. You see a lazy, meandering river, and hear the sweet sound of its constant trickle. You also see a white fabric sheet floating in front of you, just a few feet up off the earth, light as a feather. It is pure and pristine, it appears divine. Take a moment to simply observe its perfection, its enoughness, its beauty.

Now, begin to think of four people in your life who you admire, perhaps, who inspire you, and who you know support you with unrelenting and unconditional love. People who you literally trust with your life. Take a moment to see each one of their faces, to see their perfectly imperfect perfection, their enoughness, their beauty, inside and out. They are radiant in their devotion to you, in this moment, and always.

Each one of them now moves toward the white sheet. They move with grace and each reaches to take hold of a corner of the now iridescent white sheet. Together, they move toward you. You see and feel their deep compassion. They surround you and you are held sacredly in this safe place. They then bring the sheet to the soles of your feet and ever so slowly, so gently, so thoughtfully, they begin to draw the white sheet up and through your body. The white sheet begins to act like a cleansing sieve, capturing and holding those thoughts, feelings, fears, and/or perceptions that do not serve you. The thoughts that do not inspire or invigorate you, and diminish your sense of worth, value, and enoughness. The ones that impede you from rising up and into the most magnificent version of yourself possible—who it is you are truly meant to be...worthy you, authentic you, empowered you.

As the white sheet moves with ease up your body, you are feeling lighter and lighter; a sense of release, of relief, infuses each cell and layer of your being. You then feel the white sheet move through and out the crown of your head, and you have the sense the sheet must be overflowing...and so very heavy to carry. And yet, your four Beloved Souls gather it in, as if it is weightless, and they float effortlessly with it, across the ground, toward the river. Upon arrival at its bank, they set the sheet adrift in the flowing river, letting it all go; your fears, debilitating self-doubts, and self-limiting beliefs. You watch the sheet, until you can no longer see it, and you feel a profound sense of freedom overcome you.

You breathe in, you breathe out, you feel spacious and capable. Your tribe turns to face you, so much love in their eyes, smiles upon their faces, and just as they appeared to you, they begin to shift from physical form into molecular form, into energy, into rays of pure white light. You then realize you are doing the same. You feel no fear though, no sense of abandonment, only contentment and hope. You know that you may come back to yourself, back to your immense value, worth, and your beyond brilliant capacity, at will, simply by taking the time to flow through this meditation, as many times as you feel it may be helpful.

Now relax for a moment and let this revelation sink into your mind and permeate your physical body. Feel the integration, feel the wholeness of your being. Allow your fears to inspire your courage, your limiting beliefs *to empower your capacity, your clarity to bring you peace of mind. And feel gratitude for those in your life that show up for you, love and accept you, as you are, in any given moment. Store the memory of this calming vibration away within your physical tissue, so that it may be recalled in times of doubt.*

Take a deep breath in, fill your belly, your rib cage and chest, and then open your mouth, let the breath go, in a big, beautiful sigh out. Return to the fullness of your breath, deep inhale, deep exhale. Now, come back to your physical body, by beginning to move slowly, kindly, and patiently. Wiggle your fingers and toes, roll your wrists and ankles, release your jaw, soften your cheeks, give your head a gentle roll. Maybe sweep your arms slowly along the floor and reach overhead, extending from the tips of your fingers, to the tips of your toes. Big breath in, bigger breath out.

Note: This meditation is full of layers, subtle and not-so-subtle insights. I have had the greatest breakthroughs with clients who have moved through the meditation repeatedly. For example, there may be different people, pets, and entities that appear at your four corners. For one of my clients, it was the Universe holding one of the corners, for another it was her cherished cat, for another her beloved dog. With repetition, new limiting beliefs and fears can be revealed and liberated.

So, to recap, the goal is getting practiced at discerning between real threats to personal safety (you need to outrun the lion!) and perceived threats, based upon negative past experiences and assumptions. Then, it's about getting cozy with your perceived fears, acknowledging their presence, appreciating their message, and choosing to utilize them as an impetus for personal growth and getting out of your own way. It's time to surrender your self-created fears, limiting beliefs, and obstacles, so that you can actualize your highest vision possible and your full human potential. I'll say it again, you are bursting with magic, set it free unto the world!

Fill Your Tank

Create and gather simple moments of joy,
stock up on them, so you may lean into the goodness
and the discomforts with equal awareness, connection, courage,
and capacity.
Living happens here,
learning happens here,
growth happens here,
oh, and a healthy dose of magic happens here.
Lean into joy with everything you've got...fill your tank!

What do simple moments of joy look like to me? Not in any order, I savor all of these things!

- Watching my son play soccer
- A star filled sky
- A sunrise run
- Playing board games with my family
- My sister's laughter
- Sipping on my chai latte, oh, and coffee!
- Yoga on the dock, well, pretty much doing anything on or near water
- Cottage time with family and friends
- Playing chess with my mom and grilled cheese lunch (made by Gramps!)
- Road tripping anywhere
- FaceTiming with my dad

- Hiking in the woods, really just being outside in nature whenever I can
- Playing on my paddleboard
- Eating a Reese's peanut butter cup
- Coffee and conversation with dear friends
- Manicure day with my niece
- A solo dance party to my fave tunes

Your turn...what delights you?!

Move

If we stop moving, WE STOP MOVING; physically, mentally, emotionally, energetically, and soulfully.

If you are currently limited in your capacity to move, due to acute injury, chronic pain, or disease, begin your recovery journey by visualizing yourself moving in all the ways you wish to move; kindly, compassionately, patiently, and lovingly—whenever you can, wherever you can, however you can.

This is a powerful intention and scientifically proven to have the same positive impact upon your healing as the movement itself.

Invitation to Learn More about the Power of Visualization:

If you wish to learn more about this, there is a wealth of information available on the power of visualization, particularly for healing and pain recovery. To kick off your exploration, I highly recommend reading the article "Using the Mind to Heal the Body: Imagery for Injury Rehabilitation" by Dryw Dworsky, PhD, and Vikki Krane, PhD, which completely blew my mind. It emphasizes how important mental strategies can be, particularly creative visualization, in aiding the recovery process for injured athletes and individuals. It highlights that healing is both a physical and mental journey.

In their research, imagery is defined as the practice of forming mental images related to desired outcomes, and it can help you feel more in control, alleviate the repetitiveness of physical rehabilitation, and potentially enhance your healing process. Sounds a lot like a manifestation practice, doesn't it? Affirming that when spirituality meets science, magic is made! For example, studies among cancer patients reveal numerous benefits from visualizing a great outcome, such as improved mood, decreased anxiety and pain, and reduced reliance on medications—all of which are applicable to those recovering from sports and exercise injuries. Whether you are recovering from an acute injury or enduring chronic pain, and since the body-mind processes pain similarly, regardless, this revelation is a game-changer. The big lesson: *Never underestimate the power of your mind!*

The article outlines practical approaches to using imagery effectively, such as relaxing before visualization, creating vivid mental pictures, and employing all senses to enhance realism. Trying meditation, just like the ones we have explored together in this book, is a great way to get started! Visualization techniques for managing pain include imagining your tense muscles relaxing or picturing soothing environments. Additionally, healing imagery can involve personal symbols of recovery, such as visualizing broken bones mending or swollen areas detoxing.

In summary, the article advocates for the power of visualization for physical rehabilitation, illustrating that the mind can play a crucial role in healing and pain recovery. Enhance your rehabilitation experience and overall recovery outcome, by seeing and feeling your way to wellness…literally!

I invite you to explore Dworsky & Krane's Healing Imagery Script:

> Take a few deep breaths…concentrate on your breathing, feel the movements of your body…just relax, sink into the chair/couch.
>
> Now focus your attention on your hurt knee…notice what it feels like…see what it looks like, the swelling, bruising… concentrate on reducing the swelling…imagine a leak in your knee and see some of the fluid drain out…concentrate on the swelling going down…see your knee returning the its normal size…concentrate on the swelling going down…as your swelling reduces, notice your knee feeling more normal.
>
> Now turn your attention to feeling the knee getting stronger…see the ligaments coming together…feel the ligaments getting tighter, growing together…concentrate on

the fibers getting bigger, stronger, tighter...feel your knee getting stronger.

Scan the muscles around the knee...begin concentrating on your quad...relax the muscle...feel the muscle become loose and relaxed...to further relax the muscle imagine your quad being massaged...feel the muscles being kneaded...notice the relaxed feeling in your quad and all around your knee.

Notice how your knee feels...concentrate on feeling relaxed... feeling stronger...you are getting better...enjoy the feeling.[1]

I am a firm believer in the power of this healing imagery process, having utilized it myself to relieve debilitating, chronic back pain and to regain mobility. I like to think of it as the *secret sauce of healing*, a mindful edge that makes feeling good again more than possible. As such, it is a strategy I confidently share with my clients, relative to supporting their personal pain recovery and successful return to physical-mental function and freedom. It really, really works! I have joyously witnessed this many times over. So, this is your personal invitation to level up your self-healing game and tap into this potent, ever-present inner resource. Go on, get saucy with it!

---

[1] Dryw Dworsky, PhD; Vikki Krane, PhD. "Using the Mind to Heal the Body: Imagery for Injury Rehabilitation." Association for Applied Sport Psychology.

Mastery

Healing takes time and oodles of patience.

And it's not about fixing ourselves. It's about learning how to make different choices and take different actions, relative to what we know today, and the resources we have available to us in this moment.

Nor must we make all of the changes we wish to make all at once. In fact, if we attempt to do so, we are likely not setting ourselves up for success—we may become overwhelmed, our goals will start to feel unattainable, and, quite frankly, we could exhaust ourselves from the tireless "efforting."

What's the alternative? We choose to prioritize and focus upon one shift, one change, one goal at a time.

Mindfully, baby-toe stepping ourselves forward; building confidence, becoming the master of that one thing, versus the master of none, and creating positive, permanent change for ourselves.

This single victory then empowers the next opportunity, the next triumph, and it contagiously ripples out from there.

The reward = slow, steady, sustainable progress.

Healing is growth, growth is healing.

During my mental health crisis eight years ago, for the first time ever, my depression was accompanied by crippling anxiety. The thing is this, I knew depression, I had a frame of reference for it, and tools and resources to draw upon. It was something I had met and successfully moved through several times in my life. Anxiety was completely foreign to me and I had no idea what to do with it.

What I did understand was that my world was rocked because my nervous system was in turbo fight-flight mode, I did not feel safe, and I was a mess! So, before I could address any other aspect of my healing I needed to calm my nervous system way the heck down! This became my one focus and the key change I made—adopting a completely restorative yoga practice.

It was not an easy shift for me, as I typically enjoyed a more vigorous, still kind, but strong movement practice. Restorative yoga is passive, whereby gravity does the work for you. The intention behind the practice is to find grounding and stillness in shapes, supported by props, blocks, blankets, bolsters, for an extended period of time (at minimum twenty minutes) to invite a gentle release of tension physically and mentally.

In essence, this leads to turning the volume down on the sympathetic nervous system (fight-flight), and turning the volume up on the parasympathetic nervous system (rest-digest). The outcome: a slow, steady lowering of anxiety and an increasing calm and capacity. I 100 percent credit restorative yoga for helping me manage and eventually overcome my anxiety, and giving me the ability to move forward into the deeper aspects of my healing and recovery. It literally saved my life.

Looking for Proof

It's a bad day, week, month, year, but it's not a bad life.

What is it then?

It's a life.

If we are really living life, that is remaining curious, truly engaging, exploring, taking chances, we are inevitably going to experience failure, discomfort, pain, loss, and grief.

Life is joy as much as it is hurt and heartache.

It is this and that.

If we choose to gather evidence and focus solely on how it's all gone wrong, the shame and guilt we feel, our regrets, we stay stuck in the narrative of not enoughness… "I suck and what's the point of trying…again."

So we don't.

We marinate in the "Ick."

We give up and hide behind our fears and limiting beliefs.

We accept what is, we retreat.

Maybe we get sick, our minds and bodies manifesting all the stress and strain of our self-flagellation and denial.

Bottom line, we let what's been hard outweigh what's been good in our lives.

We give it more power.

So, what's the alternative?

We practice shifting our mindset.

We choose to learn from our living, to inform our decision-making through our lived experience.

We forgive ourselves for what we didn't know then.

We try again...and again...and again...and again...

We don't stop.

We keep learning, we keep growing.

We remember that joy, fulfillment, success, and expansion are just as possible (let's look for this proof, instead!), so why not choose to give more time, more energy, more power to fuel this narrative.

Leading ourselves through the ups and downs, with wisdom, intention, trust, courage, compassion, love, capacity, and resilience.

It's not a bad life.

It's your life.

It's precious.

The whole of it.

Every up and down of it.

Steps

Sometimes, we must...
step into discomfort
to find ease;
step into dysfunction
to find function;
step into chaos
to find peace;
step into vulnerability
to find strength;
step into sadness
to find joy;
step into loss
to find connection;
step into pain
to find healing;
step into darkness
to find light.

Transformation

Breathe in through your nose, feel the coolness of the air as it passes in through your nostrils. Draw the inhale into your belly, your rib cage, your chest...invite expansion.

Now release the breath in exhalation, from your belly, your rib cage, your chest, feel its warmth as it passes through the nostrils...soften, let go.

This is sustainable transformation in its simplest form...from inhale to exhale, from fullness to emptiness, from coolness to warmth, from oxygen to carbon dioxide, from nourishment to waste. All in an effort to maintain homeostasis—a stability and equilibrium of our physiological processes.

Diet, hydration, exercise, sleep, alcohol, smoking, environment, and stress, reflect a few of the factors impacting how hard the body must work to support an optimal state of being.

If balance cannot be restored over time, the body says "enough" and unattended vulnerabilities may eventually present themselves in the form of serious illness and disease.

Our mental health is no different. The fact is, like our bodies, our minds are hard-wired for change, for adaptation, and evolution. Our capacity to think, reason, and choose permits us to experiment, explore, and experience life in all its freaking glory.

We are by nature facilitators of change and sometimes the instigated shifts serve us well, and sometimes they do not. If we traverse too far along the path of self-neglect, including self-destructive thoughts and behaviors, vulnerabilities may again present themselves in the form of panic, anxiety, depression, and other mental health challenges. We then find ourselves fighting fiercely to return to a state of stability and equilibrium.

Practicing diligent self-awareness, self-acceptance, and self-care is key to managing the ebb and flow of life.

Change, welcome or not, is inevitable, and if we choose to meet it with attentiveness, kindness, compassion, and patience—we learn, we grow, we transform.

We feel good.

The Tortoise

We human beings often choose to face our challenges like a bull in a china shop…kicking doors down, in hopes it will catapult us to the other side of fear, discomfort, heartache, loss, grief, and pain.

We may also choose to self-soothe in ways that numb our feelings and deny our experience. The "soldier on" approach.

We then convince ourselves "this is coping."

Yes, it may meet our immediate needs.

Yes, it may bring us some short term relief.

But, and this can be a very BIG BUT, it may not be what serves us best in the long run.

Sometimes, what is needed is slow, steady effort in the direction we wish to go…rebuilding our capacity, inspiring confidence, gaining traction, and empowering progress.

Being the tortoise not the hare.

Not Your First Rodeo

If in your lifetime you have successfully met, managed, and moved through periods of depression and/or anxiety by making use of available resources, learned skills, and self-care strategies. YOU, resilient human, have a history of healing and recovery.

This is a very good thing and will serve you well should you find yourself immersed, once more, in deep struggle.

Gently remind yourself, this is not your first rodeo.

Trust in your capacity to survive and thrive. You have done it before, YOU WILL DO IT AGAIN.

DEEP

deep living
deep loving
deep experience
deep reward
deep scars
deep healing
deep growth
deeper living
deeper loving
deeper

B.S.

That voice in your head,
the one that says you are not good enough,
strong enough, worthy enough...yeah,
you know the one.
Go ahead, hit the mute button,
right freaking now,
knowing with your whole heart that
the only language it's fluent in is BS!

Hell & Back

We journey to hell and back,
once, twice, three times over,
only so we may return to
shine our light more brightly.
It is in these grueling,
seemingly unbearable moments of life,
that we must find the will to keep going,
to trust and believe.

You've Got This

Step aside, Sunshine, and let yourself work your magic—
you've got this.

Get out of your own way. Let go of self-judgement, feelings of not enoughness, fear, and limiting beliefs. Instead, tap into your magic (we all have it!). When we lean into our passion and purpose, we might not get it right the first time, or the second, or the third, for that matter. But each time we learn more and we refine our process until we get there!

Even if you stumble, fall, and fail, at the very least you will learn.

And when rising up and moving forward, with the invaluable insights gained, you will fight smarter for the life of your dreams.

Buried Treasure

Dive deep, deeper still, into the sometimes brilliant, sometimes tumultuous sea of life.

Get lost. Get found.

Over and over again.

Sink. Swim. Repeat.

And remind yourself, it's at rock bottom, right next to the wreckage, where the buried treasure is also discovered.

Celebrating You

I see you putting in the excruciatingly hard work.

I hear you evolving your dialogue within, from self-deprecation to self-appreciation.

I feel you filling yourself up with mind-body-soul goodness, as you move resiliently through your story.

I celebrate you, as you courageously and lovingly lead yourself into deep healing and sustainable recovery.

Keep going.

You are doing an amazing job.

Yes, it is hard work and it is the best work you will ever do.

YOU ARE WORTH IT.

chapter 4

Made for the Now

Breathe.
It may be all you can manage
in this moment,
and it is enough.
As long as we breathe,
the possibilities are endless.

Life unfolds in the present. It is a tapestry woven by single moments that invites us to expand intentionally into our lived experience, as a fully conscious, competent participant in the curation of our own lives. This is the offering and when we master mindfulness: we gift ourselves the opportunity to embrace the beauty and richness of *now*. Refining our ability to release the weight of the past and the uncertainty of the future, and unlocking a deeper connection to ourselves and the world around us. Evolving a capacity to step boldly into the present, where each heartbeat, each breath, is a chance to rediscover joy, purpose, and the profound power of simply being.

NOW

Life is happening now. It can only be actioned in the present moment. And it is here where our choices either send us soaring into a fill-your-cup orbit of goodness, or spiraling insidiously into the quicksand of slowly-draining living.

The quality of our choices determines our ability to reconcile with our past and not be held hostage by it. Alternatively, our choices can force us to stay stuck, all whilst forming and fortifying our future.

So, how do we get better at present moment awareness, connection, and action?

How do we evolve daily habits that serve our past, present, and future, and allow us to live and learn and grow through our lived experience?

We practice.

It is in the present moment we possess the greatest amount of power to choose, to problem solve, to create, to innovate, to impact, to affect change, and to take mindful, purposeful action.

Present moment processing may look like this:

Taking an intentional pause in the in-betweens of your day (I like to call them "islands of calm"), to slow down, to observe your breath, to get in touch with your senses, or lack thereof, and to notice your emotions, inner dialogue, mood, and energy. Maybe it's a moment to mindfully move in your body, to sit in gratitude, to celebrate a win, or to acknowledge a disappointment—not later, but now.

Then, receiving and utilizing these insights to move into the next part of your day on purpose, in alignment.

Gifting yourself capacity and conscious living in the now.

Leading yourself forward into deep, rich, rewarding living.

The Awe

When we find ourselves immersed in the busyness of our lives, caught in the quagmire of distraction, it's easy to overlook the magic in the mayhem of it all, the moments of wonder and enchantment weaved marvellously throughout our days.

Instead, we lead ourselves through the motions of living, consumed by our daily routines and responsibilities, forgetting to pause to recognize the miracle of simply breathing and being. We miss the exquisite artistry of watercolour skies at sunset, the contagious, tear-induced laughter shared with a loved one, or the pure pleasure of a warm breeze barely there upon our skin.

So, what if we shifted our focus from the ordinary to the extraordinary in every moment?

What if we embraced the idea that life is filled with opportunities to experience awe, even in the smallest, most subtle of things, even when we are arduously pushing through the slog of The Ick?

What if we chose to look for the yummy goodness, especially when it's heavy and hard?

Let's imagine walking through our days with eyes wide open, receptive to The Awe that unfolds around us.

What might happen?

More connection...

- To self
- To others
- To the earth
- To all its inhabitants
- To the universe

More gratitude and appreciation.

More capacity, compassion, love, and belonging.

Our lived experience is a perfectly imperfect masterpiece, painted with the most poignant, unexpected moments of beauty, whether it's a stranger's kindness, nature's resilience, or the love that flows between friends and family.

We can unlock deeper emotional experiences and richer connections by nurturing curiosity and using all our senses. See it, smell it, hear it, taste it, touch it.

Expanding our understanding of ourselves and the world around us.

It's not about ignoring adversity; it's about accepting it as a part of life, not separate from it, walking graciously with the discomfort, pain, and hardship, as you would the myriad of moments that spark delight, inspiration, and connection.

Remember we only know Awe because we know Ick.

Invitation to Lean Into The Awe:

How do you learn to hold conscious space for The Awe within and around you?

You train for it.

I encourage you to move through your days with a journal in tow for at least one week, on the ready, to record the mini and major moments of awe that pepper your day!

Get practiced at paying attention.

Write down each observation and experience.

How did it make you feel?

Did it create a shift within you, perhaps in mood, energy, or action?

At the end of the week, think about how consistently tapping into The Awe impacted your feelings of capacity, connection, and aliveness.

Keep practicing!

All Our Moments Matter

All our moments matter. It is within these moments we are gifted the opportunity to live, and love, and learn. To gain experience, to inform our choices, to decide differently, to remain curious, particularly around the tougher stuff. To take the much-needed pause we deserve, to sit in conscious awareness, to foster deep connection, to re-group, to realign...to try and try again...to grow and grow again. We are here to live, so let's!

Dear Me

I want to keep finding more compassion, acceptance, and love for who I was then, Past Me.

So, I can do better by Present Me, informed by my past, not held hostage by it, and be led forward by the wisdom I've gained through experience.

So, I can show up for Future Me with the curiosity, capacity, and grace to meet all the expressions of a life well-discovered and lived—the love and the loss, the success and the disappointment, the joy and the pain. All of it.

So, I can release the drama in favor of savoring the simplicity of quieter, steadier times that invite deeper connection, contentment, and peace.

So, I can keep exploring, keep learning, keep aligning, and keep growing.

So, I can love bigger and live my best life in the time I get to be here.

Love, Me

PS. You're doing great, keep going!

Presence

Take time each day to savor simple moments.
It is these occasions that make moving through
the tough stuff more bearable, more doable.
They inspire hope in our hopelessness.
They give rise to the courage in our fear.
They lead us out of stagnation and into expansion.
They compel us to keep going no matter what.
Choose to be fully present in these most magical moments of
your life.
This is where the feel-good lives.

Just Breathe

When it feels excruciatingly hard,
all that you need to keep going
is to keep breathing.
Possibility never ceases to exist
in your next breath,
and it is here,
in each inhale and exhale
that you have the opportunity
to lead yourself forward into new outcomes.
It is here that your healing and recovery happens,
it is here you begin to live again.

P.M.P. – Present Moment Practice

Breathe in...

root
reach
NOTICE
nudge the edges
soften
create space
CONNECT

Breathe out...

let go
surrender
RELEASE
open
heart
mind

Purposeful
PRESENT
MOMENT
practice

ALIGN
action
expand

LIVE
inspired

Just One

Sometimes all it takes to invite ease and shift energy is one mindful, beautiful breath in, followed by a long, slow, steady breath out.

Inhale.

Fill yourself up, receive the nourishment.

Exhale.

Let it all go, release what no longer serves you.

Repeat as needed.

The breath...Your Breath...is powerful.

Be present in it.

Be intentional with it.

As long as there is breath, there is hope and possibility.

What's So Great About Breath, Anyway?

I know what you're thinking, *Gosh this girl talks a lot about the breath.* Why? Because it's that damn important.

Firstly, when we breathe, we live...a major perk. And if we choose to be mindful of our breath at any given moment, life gets even better!

Attending to our breath can ease symptoms of anxiety by compelling us to remain rock solid in the present moment—not stuck in the past, beating ourselves up, or consumed by worries of an unknown future—but rather, being right here, right now.

Secondly, a single moment in time is far more manageable than many moments lumped together in one giant overwhelming clusterf*@k of regret and fear. When we are in crisis, we lack perspective.

Lastly, slowing down the breath and extending the exhalation (i.e. inhale four counts, exhale six counts) can literally shift the physiology of anxiety, by inviting ease to a ramped up nervous system, turning down the volume on fight-flight-freeze-fawn, and turning up the volume on rest-digest-rejuvenate. We can shift ourselves from heart palpitations, sweats, body tremors, and monkey-mind into greater calmness in all layers of being.

The breath: the gift that keeps on giving.

To-Do List

Self-care does not belong on our to-do list.
It is so much more than this.
It's the priority.
It's non-negotiable.
So STOP negotiating with yourself.
Choose it.
Do it.
Like your life depends on it.
Hint: It does.

Choose yourself today for healthier and happier tomorrows.

Self-Care Q & A for the Win!

What is capturing your attention?

_____
_____
_____
_____

Are you choosing it consciously?

_____
_____
_____
_____
_____
_____

On purpose?

_____
_____
_____
_____
_____

Are you looking at it through the lens of your core values?

_____
_____
_____
_____
_____

Does it feel truly aligned?

_____
_____
_____
_____

Does it allow you to be authentically YOU?

_____
_____
_____
_____

Is it taking you in the direction you wish to grow?

_____
_____
_____
_____

Asking yourself these questions on the regular and answering them, honestly, will gift you empowered feel-good living in the now.

The Special Occasion

Every day we wake up breathing with our heart beating is cause for celebration!

Yet, it's not something we tend to spend a lot of time thinking about. Unless we have been given a reason to be more thoughtful of the vitality that flows through us, perhaps, we were forced to through injury or illness, we can very easily take our well-being for granted and simply go about our business of daily doing. It becomes checking off to-do-lists, meeting expectations of ourselves and others, feeling like there are not enough minutes in the day, heightened stress, resentment, frustration, and very little room for play and pleasure. We push the feel-good stuff off, and we save the fun for later, like that expensive perfume or the fine wine for a *"special occasion."*

Not only that, pain can take over and become the Goliath, working hard to keep our joy small, and bullying happiness, pleasure, and gratitude. Overwhelming pain can blind us, deafen us to joy's presence, so we must work even harder to keep our eyes and ears open, to remind ourselves that joy continues to exist alongside our heartache. Even if it's fleeting, it offers a glimmer of light in the dark, it keeps us hoping, it keeps us living. Have you ever attended a Celebration of Life for a loved one, and, at the peak of grief, someone shares a story, recalling memories, and laughter erupts? That is joy existing alongside the heartache—this and that.

So, guess what?!

Read the very first line of this passage, again.

One more time for good measure, say it with me: *"Every day we wake up breathing with our heart beating is cause for celebration!"*

THIS is the Special Occasion!

It's like we don't feel we are worthy of experiencing delight every single day, that life is meant mostly to be a slog with a little hit of happiness here and there…if we are lucky!

This is such a disservice to ourselves and it makes moving through the tough stuff even tougher!

No more waiting.

It's time to get practiced at peppering your day with simple pleasures and *creating* intentionally joyous moments to celebrate Your Miraculous Human Experience in this exact moment of your life. Building up your Joy Reserve for those darker days.

So, right here, right now, draft your Pleasure List.

Check it once, twice, keep evolving it, and most importantly, GET TO IT!

Feel-good living is your birthright.

_____
_____
_____
_____
_____
_____

Roaming

Where mind and heart roam, energy and life flow.

Resting

It is more than OK...and necessary...to slow things down, to alternate the doing with the resting.

Savoring the beauty, the stillness, the simple things, and everything in between.

Infusing each breath, movement, thought, and feeling with gratitude for all that you are in this very moment...enough.

Expanding into your inner knowing, aligning to it.

Reminding yourself, over and over again, when all feels lost, you have the power within to find your way home.

Trusting you are *made for this*.

Pink

Living life in the pink, consistently, sustainably, despite its ups and downs, takes daily, diligent awareness and deep connection to your inner world.... breath, sensation, thoughts, feelings, mood, energy, and intuition.

Keeping your fingers on the pulse of your present moment experience.

A little tweak here.

A little tweak there.

Actioning life on purpose.

Exploring.

Engaging.

Evaluating.

Adjusting.

Adapting.

Aligning.

Realigning.

Practicing.

Playing.

Learning.

Growing.

Healing.

Evolving.

Repeating.

Intentional, conscious living and loving, at its very best.

Immerse yourself in the practice of "in the pink" empowered, feel-good living.

★

*Say the following affirmations out loud to yourself
and mean it...with your whole, open heart:*

I am enough.

I am worthy.

I matter.

★

Smile

As in right now, this very second,
allow yourself to sit in your smile,
to savour its sweetness,
to truly know and feel your joy,
this will serve you well,
when you need to remember it the most.

Fox Trot

Healing and recovery is not a linear path. In fact, it can feel more like some sort of crazy-ass square dance, that in no way, shape or form, resembles a square; one step forward, followed by two steps back, a dog leg left, then three steps right, and then spinning, definitely LOTS of spinning.

In the beginning, there is no rhythm, no groove, it's just a free-for-all of overwhelming thoughts and feelings, knee-jerk reactions and actions. Not to mention exhaustion, from efforting with everything we've got to keep it all flowin' and goin'.

We can hang out here, in some variation of this funky, little Fox Trot, for quite some time, trying to find the rhyme or reason of it all. Some days we are rockin' it, and other days we are crashin' and burnin', in some sort of dramatic, not so graceful, final act that, when all is said and done, looks and feels a whole lot like fetal position. Oh, wait a minute, that's because it is.

And it is right here, in this glorious heap of humanness, we must catch ourselves, slow it all down, curl inward a little more—not to hide, but rather to hold ourselves even tighter. To have deeper kindness, compassion, acceptance, patience, and love for ourselves. Giving ourselves an ample opportunity to reflect, to rethink, to remind—we are enough, we are worth it, we will do this, it will get better, it will not last forever, perspective will come, we will feel good again, and life will too. To reset, to reboot, to refine, to redo, and to repeat as required.

There is no rush. We must process, we must practice, we must do the inner work. NOW. If we choose not to, "IT" will find us again (fun fact!), and when it does, it will revisit with an almighty, swift kick in the caboose, mercilessly demanding our attention.

Gratitude When It's Hard

How incredibly challenging can it be to feel any connection to gratitude, when our lives have been turned upside down? When nothing makes sense. When we are suffering. When we are in the throes of healing from trauma, chronic pain, moving through loss and grieving. Under these circumstances, feeling thankful for anything can feel so out of reach, and let's be honest, freaking impossible!

Practice tips for daily gratitude when it's hard:

Appreciating Small Moments

- The sunlight streaming through a window and its warmth on your skin
- Sitting dockside listening to loons calling out on the lake

Recognizing Support

- Feeling grateful for friends and family who check in on you, even if it's simply a text or a call

Feeling Grateful for Basic Necessities

- Taking a moment to acknowledge having a warm meal, a cozy bed, and shelter from the elements

Celebrating Personal Strengths

- Reflecting on your ability to rally yourself when there is nothing left in the tank, and doing the best you can to meet each day with courage and strength, no matter how challenging it may be

Finding Comfort in Nature

- Feeling thankful for a moment spent outside, even if it's just a walk around the block to move your body and breathe in the fresh air

Valuing Creative Outlets

- Recognizing your ability to express yourself through art, writing, or music, which can provide a healthy outlet for your feelings, some relief and solace

Cherishing Memories

- Thinking of a special memory that makes you smile and reminds you of happier times, that feeling good is possible

Honouring Your Healing Progress

- Making mindful note of even the smallest steps forward, like just getting out of bed or eating breakfast, give yourself a well-deserved pat on the back

Offering Kindness to Yourself

- Thanking yourself for letting yourself rest and indulging in self-care, getting your haircut, painting your nails, having a bubble bath, taking a nap…

Finding Joy in Laughter

- Watching funny videos or your favorite comedy, sharing a joke with a friend, dancing to your favorite song like nobody's watching, letting laughter and joy flow through you, reminding yourself again that feeling good is possible

So, if gratitude is our capacity to be fully present in each moment of our lives, let's talk about living in the "What Is" moment. That is unstucking ourselves from the "What If" and living for the "What Is."

We may, at times, find ourselves held hostage by the "What If…?"

What if I don't heal?
What if you do?

What if I don't recover?
What if you end up healthier than you have ever been?

What if I fail?
What if you succeed...eventually...and it's more than you could ever have asked for?

What if it hurts?
It likely will and that's ok, trust it will begin to feel better as you reconnect, realign, and give yourself the space to heal.

What if I hurt somebody else?
What if you are actually hurting yourself more by not speaking your truth?

What if I am judged?
You just might be. Again, that's ok. If you are choosing authentically and it feels right for you, that matters more. If you hold yourself back from living your truth, in fear of what others think, down the road you will judge yourself harder than they ever could. That's called regret and it sucks!

What if I am let down?
Great! It gives you the opportunity to learn, get clearer, get up, and try again!

What if I am rejected?
Again, it can and will happen. What's more important is that you don't reject yourself. That you give yourself the space and grace to be a perfectly-imperfect human in progress; living, learning, growing, and doing better for you, first and foremost.

What if "they" come back?
They might and if they do, you get to choose, based on where you are at and what you know in that moment, to make an informed decision that makes sense for you. Maybe it's a hard no. Maybe you engage in the relationship, again, but do so with clear boundaries that honour you and them. In this way, maybe you gain the opportunity to learn and grow together.

What if "it" comes back?
It just might. If it does, it's not your first rodeo. You have experience on your side now. You can make more informed decisions. You already have resources and a toolkit at the ready that you can draw upon to lead yourself forward. It won't be easy, but you will meet it and move through it with intention and grace and love.

What if my world implodes?
It happens. It's freaking hard. Remind yourself, sometimes you have to deconstruct to reconstruct, breakdown to breakthrough. When the time comes, you will do it, you will keep going, you WILL find your way.

WHAT IF...?

All prognostications of an undetermined future, of what may or may not be, and we have absolutely no control here.

So, what if, instead, we choose to live in the "What Is" moment. As in, right now, this second...

★

I am enough.
I am open.
I am connected.
I am grounded.
I am curious.
I am creative.
I am optimistic.
I am boundless.
I am brave.
I am resilient.
I am authentic.
I am growing.
I am healing.
I am recovering.
I am love.
I am loved.
I am life.
I am gratitude.
I AM....

★

In this way, we are making a conscious choice, we are taking control, despite the chaos that may exist within and around us.

Empowering equanimity and cultivating capacity through gratitude and acceptance—while being the eye of the hurricane.

This is the practice.

Flip It

How often do you consider the depth of your own happiness, and do an intentional check in?

Daily?

Monthly?

Yearly?

At all?

Do you take time to explore your happiness, from a place of authentic awareness and relative to your core values?

Do you take time to compassionately connect to your happiness, with an open heart and open mind?

Do you consciously acknowledge opportunities for experiencing greater contentment and growth?

In so doing, you inspire aligned action, so that you may empower and compel your very own happiness. Not from a place of selfishness, but rather from a place of selflessness. When we feel good, when we feel aligned, we shine, we serve, we make a difference.

In your constant pursuit of happiness (feel free to replace the word happiness with any word that resonates for you like joy, peace, contentment…), how elusive does actualizing "it" feel, let alone establishing a committed relationship with "it"? What if you choose to flip the paradigm? What if, through your daily habits of wellness, instead of you chasing happiness, happiness was chasing you? You can, in fact, draw happiness towards you. You can feel joy, contentment, and peace, right now—TODAY. You can make it sustainable, even when life is perfectly imperfect…even when it's damned hard.

You matter.

Your happiness matters.

I invite you to take this moment to consider your happiness…yes, I do mean right now…there's no time like the present—wink wink!

This Day

today is the only day of its kind in existence

breathe in it
be in it
play in it
laugh in it
love in it
live in it
whole mind
whole heart
whole soul

you are made for the now

chapter 5

Made for Connection

In this life,
if you do anything fiercely,
make it love.

In the montage of life, our connections have the power to see us thrive. Our relationships make us richer, and allow deeper expressions of ourselves. Yet, if misaligned, they can bring us to our knees and make us feel less than, lost, and strangers to ourselves. Embracing the ecstatic joy and the heart-crushing pain that inevitably accompanies our most meaningful relationships offers the most invaluable insights about love, loss, boundaries, and resilience. Relationships remind us we can survive and thrive, especially when love hurts and feels impossibly hard. First and foremost, we must learn to nurture a healthy connection with ourselves. We must foster a solid foundation from which we can intentionally and constructively engage with others and create mutually rewarding and respectful bonds. The kinds where spirits feel nourished and everyone flourishes.

Self-Love and Boundary Meditation

Begin by finding a comfortable position, either seated or lying down. Close your eyes gently and take a deep breath in through your nose, filling your lungs completely. Hold that breath for a moment. Now exhale slowly through your mouth, releasing any tension you may feel. Do this a few more times, allowing your breath to flow naturally and effortlessly.

As you settle into your space, set an intention for this meditation. You might say to yourself, "In this moment, I choose to honor and love myself unconditionally." Allow this intention to radiate into your heart and out into the entirety of your being.

Now shift your awareness to your body. Starting from the top of your head, slowly scan down to your toes. Notice any areas of tension or discomfort, and breathe into those spaces. With each exhale, imagine releasing that tension, allowing your body to relax further.

Now, in your mind's eye, visualize a warm, golden light surrounding you. This golden glow represents your capacity for self-love. Imagine it growing and flowing into your body with every inhale, filling you with compassion and grace, illuminating every part of you, getting brighter and brighter, reminding you that you matter.

As you continue to breathe deeply, begin to repeat the following affirmations silently or aloud:

- I honor my needs and desires.
- I am worthy of love and respect.
- It is okay to say no.
- My boundaries protect my well-being.

Feel the empowering energy of these words as you reinforce your commitment to yourself.

Now, bring to mind your relationships. Visualize each one you hold dear. Imagine setting healthy boundaries in these relationships, ones that align with your self-worth and values. See yourself communicating your needs and desires clearly and authentically and upholding these boundaries, especially when they are being challenged. Allow yourself to sit in the feelings that rise up for you.

Breathing in, fill yourself up with confidence and conviction.

Breathing out...let go of any fear and confusion.

Now, shift your focus to gratitude. Think of three things you appreciate about yourself. These could be qualities, achievements, or aspects of your personality. Let yourself bask in this feeling of gratitude and nourish your sense of self-love. Take a few more deep breaths, bringing your awareness back to your body and the present moment. When you're ready, gently wiggle your fingers and toes, and open your eyes.

Before you fully return to your day, take a moment to reflect on how you can anchor this more deeply rooted self-love in every single cell of your being, and how you may integrate the consistent practice of healthy boundaries into your daily life.

Carry this intention with you to guide, support, and inspire your relationship interactions moving forward.

Now, a little pause to thank yourself for taking this time to nurture and honor your relationship with the most important person in your life...you! And reminding yourself that every intentional action you take towards loving yourself more and establishing healthy and firm boundaries is a leap forward in cultivating more mutually authentic, meaningful and rewarding relationships.

Heartbeat

Love is held in this space,
a kind, compassionate, patient, soulful,
determined, boundless, timeless,
unconditional kind of love,
it lives and breathes here,
with its very own heartbeat.

Love Note to Self

I only ever wanted to love you.
I only ever will.
Even when it hurts and is the hardest.
Because loving you should be
the easiest thing I ever do...
not the hardest.

Cause & Effect

What do you think would happen
if you devoted time each day
to intentionally loving yourself more?

Ripples

The aligned decisions that feel
the heaviest, the hardest, and the
scariest to act on, often hold the
greatest potential for the deepest
levels of healing, loving, and living—
for myself and for those with whom
I share a connection.

Here

be and breathe
live and love
present in each moment
islands of calm
mindful awareness
deep connection
inspired intention
aligned action
empowered living
your birthright
you are the magic you seek

Somebody

We all want to feel like
somebody to someone,
and that begins with
being that somebody to ourselves.

Somebody to me,
to be somebody to you,
to be somebody to each other.

All of It

Love yourself through,
the good stuff, the tough stuff,
the pretty bits, the ugly bits,
bottom line,
love yourself.

What if you devoted the next 365 days to loving yourself more?

Love Yourself More Meditation

Find a quiet space where you can sit comfortably or lie down. Allow your body to relax and your mind to settle. This meditation is designed to help you cultivate self-love, especially during challenging times.

Close your eyes gently. Take a deep breath in through your nose, filling your lungs completely. Hold it for a moment, and then exhale slowly through your mouth. Let go of any tension you may be holding. Repeat two more cycles of this deep breathing, feeling a sense of calm wash over you with each breath out.

Step 1: Acknowledge Your Feelings

As you continue to breathe deeply, bring your awareness to your heart space. Notice any emotions that arise—both positive and negative. It's okay to feel a mix of emotions, especially during more challenging times. Acknowledge these feelings without judgment. Say to yourself, "I honour my feelings, and I am here for myself."

Step 2: Embrace Your Whole Self

Visualize yourself as a whole person, encompassing all the good, the not-so-good, your favorite parts, and your perceived imperfections. Imagine wrapping your arms around yourself in a warm embrace. Whisper softly to yourself, *"I love you. All of you."* Feel the warmth of this love spreading throughout your body into every cell of your being. Flood your whole self with this love.

Step 3: Commit to Small Acts of Self-Care

Now, think about small actions you can take daily to show up for yourself. Picture yourself doing these little things: enjoying a warm cup of tea or coffee, taking a few moments to breathe deeply under a tree or in the sun, writing down three things you appreciate about yourself, indulging in a hobby that brings you joy, even if just for a few minutes, speaking kindly to yourself, especially when you feel down. As you visualize these moments, breathe in the intention to care deeply for yourself and breathe out any negativity or self-doubt.

Step 4: Seek Stillness and Reflection

Now, picture yourself sitting in a serene environment where you feel safe, whether it's a tranquil forest, a quiet beach, or a cozy room. Spend a few moments reflecting on the times you've struggled. Remind yourself that it's okay to face difficulties and that you are not alone in this journey. Affirm silently, *"No matter what, I am deserving of love and understanding."*

Step 5: Create Your Daily Intentions

With love and compassion for yourself, think of one intention you can set for the day ahead. It may be something like *"I will treat myself with kindness"* or *"I will pause and take care of my needs."* Hold this intention close to your heart; let it serve as a touchpoint to remind you of your promise to love yourself as you meet and move through the ups and downs of your day. Let it inspire aligned action and the necessary course corrections in your day, that prioritize choosing you and giving yourself what you need. This is self-love and self-respect.

Conclusion

Begin to bring your awareness back to the present moment. Wiggle your fingers and toes, feeling the earth beneath you. When you are ready, gently open your eyes. Take a moment to notice how you feel. Remember, you can return to this meditation whenever you need a reminder to *love yourself more*. As you move through your day, carry this abundance of self-love within you. Allow it to guide your decisions, thoughts, and interactions. You are worthy of love - every moment, every day. Self-love is nurtured in the little things you do each day and amplified through consistent practice, you declaring to yourself, over and over again, "I am worth it, and I matter."

364 days to go!!! You got this!!!

Hearts

Home is where my heart is,
your home is where your heart is,
when hearts are shared
truthfully, respectfully, tenderly,
in such nourishing conditions,
love expands exponentially
and anything becomes possible.

In the Quiet

Acts of great love
are often unseen,
happening without declaration,
without fanfare,
arriving to us in unexpected,
perhaps, unrecognizable ways,
packaged differently,
given and received in the quiet,
in the softest subtleties of the
deepest human connection.

Breadcrumbs

Repeat after me:

I will no longer
give all of myself,
over and over again,
for breadcrumbs,
over and over again.

This is not a
healthy relationship,
this is not balanced,
mutually rewarding
and respectful love,
it is conditional love,
it is unfulfilling love,
it is lonely love.

I love you _____. (person's name)
I love myself more.

Because

You lost her.

Not because she doesn't love you.

Because she does.

It's because,
for all of your love,
she feels worthless.

It's because,
with this realization,
she is remembering
who she *was* before you,
enough.

And because she is reminded,
with self-compassion and patience,
practice and time,
she will be ok,
because she returns to
finding value in herself.

Eventually,
she will be MORE than ok,
because she now knows,
first and foremost,
she is her everything.

Aligned Love

When my love expands from the deepest
self-awareness and connection,
my values uncompromised,
I can practice aligned love for you,
compassionately and respectfully,
without resistance and resentment,
walking with you on your life journey,
honoring my boundaries, and yours,
rooted in my truth, in my integrity,
loving you through,
authentically,
boundlessly.

Love is Life

It is kindness and it is patience
It is compassion and it is passion
It is non-judgement and it is acceptance
It is within us and it surrounds us
It is self-care and it is selfless
It is listening and it is letting go
It is lost and it is found
It is exquisite and it is excruciating
It breathes and it inspires
It honors and it heals
It is giving and it is receiving
At its very best it is unconditional
Love is life

Love is My Only Language

Perfectly-imperfectly, to the best of my ability, I traverse this life through the lens of love.

Love leads me...
my breath
my heart
my mind
my energy
my soul

Ever grateful to love and be loved.

Precipice

Hand in hand
precipice
one breath
one moment
one step
one leap
free fall
together apart
bound forever
always love
infinite life

Cosmos

You breathe and are
in my every heartbeat,
without condition,
beyond space, time, and reason,
tethered stars,
dancing in the cosmos.

Truth

Love is,
has always been,
will always be,
my truth.

Oxygen Mask

I must know how to show up, support, love,
and walk with myself well, if I wish to show up,
support, love, and walk with you well.

You must know how to show up, support, love,
and walk with yourself well, to show up,
support, love, and walk with me well.

I will put my oxygen mask on first,
so I can be there for me and you.

You put yours on first,
so you can be there for you and me.

Together, we will graciously, courageously,
and resiliently traverse this life.

How Do I Love Me?

The depth and quality of your relationships directly reflect your capacity to honour and love yourself, first and foremost, unconditionally. When you get well-practiced at placing value on your own needs and desires, not just prioritizing everybody else's (yes, I am talking to you!), you are setting high standards for yourself. These standards elevate your self-worth and, at the same time, set the bar for what treatment you are willing to tolerate from others. Guess what we are talking about here? Yep, you got it, insert the B word here—boundaries—are an act of profound self-love that says, "I matter, too. What you are asking of me is not in alignment with my values, nor is it respectful of my time or energy level right now, or...."

And what happens if you consistently choose to compromise your well-being for the sake of another? You betray yourself (big time!) and hold the door wide open for those relentless Boundary Breachers in your life. The risk? Over time, this constant self-neglect will deplete you, maybe even make you sick. Consider this your loving invitation to STOP.

So, what's the takeaway? If you crave mutually rewarding, respectful, authentic relationships, prioritize building a relationship of integrity with yourself, get super clear on your non-negotiables, speak up and ask for what you need, and lead others through the consistency of your choices and actions. Remember, boundaries are not unidirectional—they go both ways. Herein lies the opportunity to create thriving relationships where you learn how to love yourself and others better. That's a win-win.

Touchpoint

Checking in...

on our sad friends, on our happy friends, and everyone in between

life is hard, it hurts, it can leave us feeling hopeless, helpless, alone

with open hearts and open minds, we become practiced at seeing the wholeness of the person standing before us

asking the tough questions

listening deeply to the answers, with empathy, compassion, patience, and love

holding safe space for vulnerable and real conversation

being fully present through the joy and the despair

not to fix, but to share the journey

helping each other access the right professional care and support when needed

this is the human experience

to feel connected

to feel seen and heard

to love and be loved

to matter

Never Give Up

Love, like humans, is perfectly imperfect.
If we give up on love, we give up on humanity.
Never give up.

Love, like humans, is perfectly imperfect. At its very best, love leads us into our most exquisite and meaningful moments of living, and, well, from there, as they say, "it's complicated." We meet ourselves and each other as we are, works in progress, shaped by birth, generations before us, geography, circumstances, childhood, our parents, siblings, friends, teachers, community, and the world today as we know it. This is just the shortlist. At the core of it all is love. It brings us together, and it pulls us apart. It can single handedly break us or repair us. And we can't live without it, we aren't meant to.

Connection is as necessary to our survival as the air we breathe and the blood that runs in our veins. We often wonder, *why are we here?* What is this earth experience really all about? Honestly, to love and be loved. That's it. It's fortune cookie material—ha! ha! And yet, we make it so freaking hard, attaching expectations and parameters to it that seemingly make us somehow more lovable, and then we spend much of our lives in the pursuit of being more lovable. *I will love myself more if... They will love me more if...* And guess what this fuels? We come to believe we are fundamentally flawed. We feed our insecurities and vulnerabilities. We incite fear in ourselves and each other. Yep, when we strive for perfection this is the proverbial baggage we amass and carry with us, and there is nothing heavier. We all suffer under its massive weight.

So, what if we collectively choose to lay the burden down? We all decide to high-five, perfectly-imperfectly, and we radically accept that love just is. A given. We don't need to earn it. It doesn't ebb and flow; it's a constant universal force within and around us, and it is meant for us all...every living, breathing entity on this planet. And that, lucky us, we get to know love in our very first breath, every breath since, and in our last breath.

Love itself is challenged by the situations we find ourselves in and our state of readiness for meeting and moving through relationships at any given time. Love is easy and spacious when it feels in alignment. But when we encounter difficulties in love—whether with partners, family, or friends—we may blame, resent, leave or simply give up. What if what's required is to evolve the expression of love in a way that honours who we are in this moment of our lives. Love, like humanity, is not static. It is fluid. A perpetual cycle of learning, growing, healing, and transforming. If we consider that we are all, in essence, explorers, here to embark on this adventure of life and love, doing the best we can with our knowledge and experience to date, it becomes easier to accept that sometimes love inevitably leads us in different directions, away from one another. This is ok. Love hasn't failed. This is love, too; spacious, and gracious, and forgiving.

If we give up on love, we give up on humanity. Love connects us; it is the thread that weaves our stories and ancestry together, enriching our lives and inspiring us to grow. Every time we find ourselves chest-deep in heartache, we learn more about ourselves, we get more intentional, and we refine how we wish to experience love moving forward. We also cultivate a greater capacity for empathy and compassion - qualities that nourish a thriving world. And needed now more than ever.

It may not always be smooth sailing, but love teaches us how to be better humans. It humbles us, reminding us that no one human is more worthy of love than another, that each of us is love and that we are all connected in love. And that we must never give up on it. EVER. In fighting for love, we acknowledge our shared bond and affirm our commitment to nurturing a kinder, more understanding world.

It will most certainly be love leading the charge if humanity and the earth are to be saved.

When love prevails, we all do.

Fall in Love

Hold yourself always in the highest esteem.
Fall madly, deeply, unwaveringly in
love with yourself, especially when it's hard.

The Mostest

Love yourself the mostest.
Why?
Because you are a walking, talking
miracle of awesomeness.
Because nobody is more worthy
of your fabulous, fierce love.
That's why!

Loving yourself the *mostest* is the real flex; it's a life-changing mindset that allows you to celebrate your individuality and leverage it to live to your fullest potential.

Why prioritize self-love?

Well, that's easy!

Because you are a walking, talking miracle of awesomeness, bursting with qualities and talents that make you uniquely YOU—it's the truth!

Yes, you are so good at acknowledging everyone else's amazingness. But let's face it, where you are really skilled is overlooking your own—dismissing and diminishing it every chance you get. And you live in a world determined to keep you stuck in comparison mode, questioning your enoughness, plagued by self-doubt, and feeling like an imposter in your own skin. Thanks, social media!

Hear me now!

Nobody and nothing else determines your worth.

You do.

YOU DECIDE.

Loving yourself is a choice that belongs to you, always.

So, ditch the soul-sucking, time-consuming, energy-wasting distractions and white noise that robs you of your inherent human value. By virtue of breathing and being on this planet, you are a mind-blowing freaking marvel of magnificence!

How does knowing this make you feel?

And as for all the other magic that makes you, well, YOU, it's the bonus material you get to play with to inspire a life of presence, purpose and passion—the bells and whistles, so to speak.

You recognize your worth when you invest your time and energy in what nourishes versus compromises your whole being. This is self-love. When you get really good at it, you are no longer battling yourself and seeking validation from others; you become your very own champion. The beautiful thing about this is it's highly contagious. Leading yourself forward in such a deeply connected way gives permission for others to do the same.

Like everything, it takes practice to make these kinds of shifts, so try out this exercise to strengthen your self-love muscle:

Take a moment to reflect on what makes you special.

Now, grab your notebook and write down at least ten qualities, achievements, or experiences that showcase your awesomeness. Everything and anything goes! Also, consider your kindness, creativity, or strength in overcoming obstacles you faced while in pursuit of these life highlights.

Notice how bringing awareness to these things makes you feel in your mind and body.

Once you have your list, stand in front of a mirror, look yourself in the eyes, and affirm these qualities aloud with conviction, "I am capable, I am creative, I am deserving of love." Let these words resonate within you.

By internalizing your worth, you transform how you see yourself and how the world perceives you, radiating confidence, love, and possibility in everything you do.

P.S. Revisit your list often. Add to it; as you grow, it grows!

Meet You There

I can't fix it.
I can't take away your pain.
I can't save you.
I wish I could.
But I will see you, hear you, and walk with you.
I will meet you there and love you through it.

Pieces

When my empathy does not include myself, and I constantly prioritize other's feelings, fears, discomfort, pain, values, goals, wants, desires, and dreams, above my own and at my expense, I inevitably give pieces of myself away.

I give my time away.
I give my energy away.
I give my worth away.
I give my self-respect away.
I give my truth away.
I give my integrity away.
I give my voice away.
I give my power away.
I give my love away.
I give my life away.
I will no longer choose this.
I will no longer abandon myself.
I will choose empathy that sees, hears, and honors both you and me in this relationship.
So we do better by each other.
Living, loving, learning, authentically, in deep connection.

Setting healthy boundaries is an act of love. A form of respect, for self, for others.

Masterpiece

We all have a highlight reel, a lowlight reel, a fall flat on your face reel.

If we are deeply diving into this adventure called life, this is the resultant reality.

It is also what makes us both the protagonist and antagonist of our very own masterpiece in the making.

Each one of us a rich, complex character, immersed in our very own narrative, of love, loss, heartbreak, grief, joy, vulnerability, strength, fear, courage, confusion, clarity, emotionality, rationality, irrationality, spontaneity, mystery, maybe even a little madness, and definitely never-ending intrigue.

It is in the genuine sharing of our stories, the good, the bad, and the downright ugly, that we have the capacity to empower deeper connection, compassion, empathy, and belonging.

Our well-being is inextricably linked to the quality of our human connections. So, aim for emotionally rich and real, mutually respectful and rewarding.

Good Vibes

Yep, if you're reading this, it's too late. I've already sent good vibes your way. They're coming and there's absolutely nothing you can do to stop them…just kick back and receive!

I Am Here

It will be ok at some point,
but right now, it's not,
and that's OK.

When we are in the throes of struggle, being told, "It's going to be ok," or "Pull up your bootstraps and soldier on" may not be exactly what we need to hear, despite good intentions.

In reality, these statements may serve to diminish our current experience, which is so far from OK, and, in that moment, seemingly impossible. We are then left feeling unseen and unheard, with our pain invalidated.

Alternatively, simple, powerful statements like "I am so sorry you are going through this" and "I am here" serve to acknowledge and hold space for a fellow human's present moment of pain, to support progressive healing, recovery, and growth.

Kind, important reminder: we don't need to show up "to fix," we simply need to show up—consistently, authentically, and with love.

Heh, You Awesome Human...

I know how hard the hard days can be, but I also know you have the will, strength, and grace to move through it, to greet a brand-new day.

I believe in you.

You

You are strength and perseverance.
You are gifted, talented,
and creative beyond measure.
You are inspiration.
You are infinite magic.
Trust. Believe.
I believe in you,
today, everyday,
always.

★

Free to Be Me Affirmation

Repeat after me…

I connect daily to the tender whispers of my heart and to the pull of my deepest inner knowing. I build an unshakeable faith in myself, so that I may courageously speak my truth. I lead myself intentionally into this day, with love, wisdom, and boundless curiosity. In this way, I am free to be me.

★

Surfing

I bask in the deep blue sea of you,
surfing the bliss of your breath, body, and being,
never lost, only ever found.

Miracle

When she loves,
and is loved,
so deeply,
so profoundly,
she recognizes the rarity of such
a precious and sacred human exchange,
she revels in its pureness,
in the miracle of its divine existence.

When he loves,
and is loved,
so deeply,
so profoundly,
he recognizes the rarity of such
a precious and sacred human exchange,
he revels in its pureness,
in the miracle of its divine existence.

When they love,
and are loved,
so deeply,
so profoundly,
they recognize the rarity of such
a precious and sacred human exchange,
they revel in its pureness,
in the miracle of its divine existence.

Two hearts,
bound,
resolutely,

throughout time and space,
no beginning,
no ending.
only,
ever more,
ever after,
ever always.

Beacon

Our love is the stillness,
the soothing calm in the chaos.

Our souls know this resolutely
and never fail to lead us home,
a precious beacon of light,
of infinite hope and possibility.

We are so much more than the darkness.

This is the strength of our love.

This is the magic of us.

Afterlife

I loved you before *I* even knew I loved you.
It has always been, it will always be.
Into the afterlife, *you and me.*

Super-Duper Juicy Bits

It hurts and it heals,
life in all its freaking glory.

When we choose to be human fully and completely, we invite both possibility and vulnerability, connection and disconnection, joy and suffering, love and loss. We hurt, we heal, we adjust, we adapt, we learn, we grow, we transform, we gain clarity, and we get real.

The reward?

Life gets richer.

As far as we know, it's a one-shot deal, so dive deep, deeper still, into the super-duper juicy bits of being.

Laugh fully.

Love fiercely.

Live wholly.

A Personal Note from Julie

Perhaps you noticed a transition in my writing in Chapter Five, as in, it is more poetic and symbolic in nature. I feel it's worth sharing the why behind this with you.

This book was written over an eight year period and reflects my own recovery journey, beginning in the acutest stages of my depression and anxiety. Yep, knee deep in The Big Ick, encumbered by a very fluid combination of confusion, chaos, overwhelm, numbness, grief, shame, and unworthiness. Everything felt hard, heavy, complicated, and murky. Like living in the heaviest fog and not being able to see or feel a thing. Stuck in my head, in my heart. And then, as if out of nowhere, the floodgates opened.

Words began to pour out of me, literally in downloads. On repeat. I took my thoughts and learnings to paper. I ruminated. I desperately and tenaciously received and worked through the ever-flowing tumble of words rising up and out from my most inner voice. I became practiced at doing so with greater self-awareness, connection, compassion, and understanding. Tenderly peeling back the layers of discomfort and pain, to find myself, to refine and reveal my truths, to heal well and wholly. I feel you can really see this process (and me!) evolving in chapters one through four, and then leading me, page by page, back into The Awe.

Cue, Chapter Five, Made for Connection. By this point my mind was free, my heart was open, my body was at peace. I felt both connected and ready for connection. There was a newfound clarity, a joyous return to creativity, and, yes, less noise. Instead, more poetic and symbolic words flowed through me. I was home.

You may also discover that once you move through the deep muck of healing, there comes this point where things become clearer for you, too. There will be less noise, and more joy. You will begin to reinhabit your senses; seeing, hearing, and feeling, again, as if for the very first time. And, when you lean into this more, it snowballs into, you guessed it, MORE! You bear witness to your apathy and detachment morphing into curiosity and connection. You become the courageous calm in the chaos. You find freedom living in your aligned authenticity.

YOU ARE MADE FOR MORE.

My wish for you is that you see and feel the very tangible possibilities of choosing yourself and the work of healing.

I know you can do it and I'm with you all the way!

Afterword

As we reach the final pages of *Made for This: Words to Thrive by When Life Gets Hard*, I would like to reflect on our shared journey. This book is more than a collection of thoughts; it is a heartfelt conversation woven with threads of experiences and lessons learned through the highs and lows of life. Each word is written with intention, serving as a beacon of hope and a trusted guide for navigating uncertainty.

Together, we took the courageous deep dive into the dualities that define our existence, the soaring moments of euphoric wonderment juxtaposed with the soul-shattering setbacks and insufferable sadness. In embracing both The Awe and The Ick, we've come to recognize the beauty in our struggles and the power in our resilience and that life is a balance of these opposing forces. It's in their moderation that we discover our strength and limitless capacity for growth.

My wish is that these pages serve as a constant reminder that you are not alone, ever. Whether standing at a crossroads or wrestling with self-doubt and despair, know that you are in compassionate company…we are all in the unending process of finding our way in this world. Embody the fundamental belief that within you lies the ability to inspire possibility, reclaim your narrative, and fall more authentically and passionately in love with yourself every single day. That when you nourish a rich relationship with yourself, you build the very best foundation for evolving a life of purpose, freedom, and fulfillment.

May you carry with you the resonating gems of insight gathered from this book. May you revisit them often and as needed. May they help you feel braver in the face of life's disquiet and allow you to trust that your boundless becoming lives and breathes in every challenge you meet, move through, and expand beyond. And remember these words remain here for you, always, to inspire and uplift you. They will bring you home and remind you that resilience is not just an outcome, but is fortified through daily habits of wellness and unrelenting self-love.

It has been such a great privilege to walk with you in these pages and share in your journey. I am so deeply grateful for your presence and hope our time together finds you living with newfound courage and grace. May you continue to thrive in the good bits and find peace amidst adversity. Never forget:

You are worthy.
You matter.
I am always here for you.

Connect with me here:
IG & TikTok: @jtwriteslife

YOU
ARE
MADE
FOR
THIS.

Acknowledgments

I've loved.
I've been loved.
I've let go.
I've been let go.
I've found.
I've lost.
And always,
I remain
anchored
in love.

This book was written because of love. Love has been my greatest teacher. I've found myself bursting in The Awe of it, and at times breaking in The Ick of it. Born with an empathy and sensitivity that nearly killed me several times over, and struggling to make sense of a world where pain and suffering give peace and joy a real run for their money, I remain here breathing, being, anchored in love.

In fact, despite being loved and let go, found and then lost, there has only ever been *more love*. The recognition that each one of us is an explorer on this earth, here to live, learn, love, grow, informed by what we know in any given moment, doing the best we can to be in relationship with ourselves and others. No real handbook, guided by gut feelings, a little luck, a Hail Mary here and there, and, well, a pathological hope—all of us just trying to figure it the heck out! And it's hard.

It is this realization that has led me into love expanding, into forgiving—myself, others—into feeling compassion over resentment, into finding clarity in the confusion, into making peace with the pain, into setting myself free, others, to keep adventuring in this experience of life, to stay curious, open, and to keep going, no matter what.

Love, always more love.

It is in the spirit of love that I share the following acknowledgements.

Firstly, I would like to take this opportunity to honour my Aunt Gay, whom we lost this past year. Speaking of a walking, talking miracle of awesomeness! She was challenged to the nth degree in her life, plagued by more aneurysms than Planters have peanuts, and according to doctors, an absolute wonder she survived the first, let alone their relentless repeat performances and complications. Their occurrences stripped her of so much, and yet, in light of it all, her will to live, her spirit, her love, her sense of humour (this!) just got bigger. I can honestly say I have never witnessed more resilience. She just never gave up!

I learned so much from you, Aunt Gay, and am ever grateful for the special relationship we shared. I always felt seen, heard, and understood when I was with you, and deeply loved. I can hear you saying to me, "Ahhhh, there's my girl." You were so full of love, and you gave it unconditionally. You spoke your truths, at times to the discomfort of others. You were unapologetically you, authentic to your core, fiercely devoted to your family and friends, and adapted to life's curveballs with an adeptness known to few. You found a way to make life work, to find joy in it, no matter what. You laughed and you kept us all laughing. You were a warrior of the perfectly imperfect, exemplifying how to meet and move through The Awe and The Ick of life with a ridiculously beyond abundance of grace and gratitude. It was such a wonderful privilege to do life with you. I am convinced you were an angel walking this earth and that your wings have now completely unfurled in all their exquisite glory, and that you are at peace, flying high with Sweetie, still laughing, and keeping all your angel friends on their toes! I miss you and I love you.

Mom and Dad, thank you for this life. I feel like I am equal parts of you both, which has been such a beautiful gift and a source of the more challenging push-pull tension of being me (acknowledged with love). Learning how to moderate my empathy and high sensitivity, to be the responsible keeper of it, and balancing my science brain, with the more esoteric, conscious, creative parts of myself. At times, I have felt like the black sheep in the family. More recently, Mom, you corrected me and said, more like the "pink sheep", and well, that just made me burst. Thank you for that. I love you both so much. I would pick you as my parents over and over again.

My siblings. Sara. Garrett. We are each other's ride or die. Sara, you are the glue, which makes sense, middle child. I like to make you laugh, because your laugh is literally one of my most favorite things on this planet. Your sense of humor and devotion to those you love is EPIC. Garrett, the fact that you went to surf your ass off in Australia, in your words "to live where people vacation," is so brave, and such an inspiration, because I know what it took for you to do so, what it has cost, and what you have gained in doing so. You have worked hard to carve out a life that feels good for you, peaceful, and this makes my heart happy. And Jo, I'm so grateful that you and G found each other. Sara Bunting and Garrett Norman, just know your big sister is so proud of you both and she loves you so much.

June 2, Lee, Carol, my beloved stepparents. Man, did we hit the jackpot with the three of you! Todd Douglas, brother-in-law extraordinaire, I'm so grateful for all that you are, all that you have overcome, all that you contribute to this family, and for loving my sister like there is no tomorrow. John and Rich, bestest brothers-in-law, I cherish you both. John and Wendy, my adored in-laws. We lost you this past year, John, but I am so, so grateful for our visit last spring. My stepsisters, Tara and Daina, I'm grateful to you for being part of my dad's life. My nieces and nephews—our oh-so-awesome next gen—Abi, Ry, Grayson, Albee, Olivia, Roxy, Gracie, Matilda, Brooklyn, Keston, Joseph, and Raf, what a gift to see you shine in this world! Love you all!!!

A.P., thank you for loving me through The Awe and The Ick. You have been there and stood by me in some of the darkest times of my life. Our path has not been an easy one. Suffice it to say, we have challenged each other on every level. Yes, I'm smiling as I write this. There is much to be said for the resilience and the love that lives between us. We have shared incredibly joyous times over the past twenty-two years with cherished family and friends, making unforgettable memories. A highlight, of course, is the birth of our boy. By far our greatest masterpiece. And you are the most amazing Dad!

Ollie, my boy. My love, my light. You. I could literally write a book on all the ways you have touched and transformed my soul over the past twenty years. I see you, I hear you, I hold you, and still there are days I pinch myself, awe-struck that you picked me as your mother, us, as your parents. Witnessing you grow into the human you are today has been such an extraordinary privilege. Kindness and love flow through you. You care deeply about the world, the people in it, and your loyalty to family, friends, and teammates is everything! I cannot wait to see what's next for you, as you continue to pursue your dreams and inspire the life you desire. Keep shooting for the stars, my love, we are with you every step of the way! I love you soooo much, plus MORE.

I honour my treasured grandparents and ancestry—Paton, Baxter, Thayer, and Lancaster. I'm grateful for this melding of lineage that has gifted my existence and the blood that runs in my veins. I feel you all in every beat of my heart.

To my dear friends, near, far, past, present, and future, you have a forever home in my heart. You have enriched my life and helped this extreme introvert find safety and comfort in connection. The journey has been easier and better for your presence in my life. I love you all.

To my clients, thank you for trusting me to walk with you on your journey of healing and recovery—for teaching the teacher. I have learned so much from each one of you. You are all co-authors of this book and I am filled with gratitude for your invaluable contribution. You are loved and celebrated, always!

To my peers, teachers, coaches, mentors, and community, you have my eternal gratitude. They say it takes a village, it truly does.

To Natasha and Morgane, this book is the very best version of itself because of you two. As they say, teamwork makes the dream work! Thank you from the bottom of my heart for contributing your endless wisdom, creativity, and expertise to this labour of love. I'm beyond grateful our worlds collided.

And lastly, most importantly, for the gift of knowing the deepest, truest love of a lifetime, I say, "Thank You." It makes surviving and thriving the hurts and heartaches more than worth it.

At the end of a day...at the end of a life...love is *everything*.

Love and more love,
Julie xo

About the Author

Inspired by her own intense healing journey—both physical and spiritual—Julie Thayer has found her calling in sharing her insights and acting as a trusted, caring guide for others. She has overcome severe depression, anxiety, and chronic pain with a variety of tools she seeks to share with the world. Using her powerful Pain Recovery Blueprint™, she has helped women across the globe do the same with their own chronic pain. She is also the founder of RECLAIMED: The Mastery™, an immersive, one-to-one coaching experience designed to help women take back their lives and feel good again.

Through her work, Julie Thayer has become a celebrated Yoga & Pain Recovery Coach and author who has successfully led hundreds of women around the world through their healing journeys and into feel-good living. Her published works aim to make healing accessible to all, no matter where they live or where they are at in their own journey.

Her first published work—*Reclaimed!: A Transformative Yoga And Self-Care Guide For Women's Empowered Healing*—aims to tackle healing through a holistic approach. Her latest work *Made for This: Words to Thrive By When Life Gets Hard* is courage transformed into words. It is designed to capture insights gained in the trenches of healing, to meet people where they are at, and to show them that even though healing can be messy and difficult, it is always worth it. This book is a culmination of her own healing experience and that of the inspiring, courageous women with whom she has had the privilege of walking the path of recovery. Every word has been written with love; in the deepest hope the passages resonate with readers and remind them...*You Are Made for This.*

www.ingramcontent.com/pod-product-compliance
Lightning Source LLC
Chambersburg PA
CBHW020522080526
44583CB00013B/696